GASTRIC BAND HYPNOSIS

HOW TO DESTROY FOOD CRAVINGS AND MELT YOUR FAT AWAY WITH EASE, WITHOUT SUFFERING THROUGH ANOTHER DIET OR EXPENSIVE SURGERY

MELANIE BOWMAN

CONTENTS

DISCLAIMER

Before we get started, I would like to inform you chapter 5 and 6 are actual hypnosis sessions that are meant to be listened to and not read. If you would like to partake in a gastric band hypnosis session, I would recommend you to grab a copy of the audio version of this book.

INTRODUCTION

"The greatest discovery of my generation is that a human being can alter his life by altering his attitudes of mind."

WILLIAM JAMES

Are you looking for more options to lose weight? Have you tried dieting and exercising, but nothing seemed to yield permanent progress? Are you reluctant to undergo gastric surgery? If so, this book is for you!

This book delves deeper into weight gain and obstacles to losing weight permanently. In this book, you'll find out why diet and exercise aren't enough for permanent weight loss, and how (and why) gastric band hypnosis can help.

Are you struggling to lose weight and keep the weight loss long-term? If so, you're not alone! Did you know that 56.4% of women and 41.7% of men in the US struggle to lose weight? Over 80% of people who've successfully lost weight eventually regain the weight, or end up being even larger than before they started the diet. Obesity is common and affects almost 50% of US Americans, with nearly $150 billion being spent on obesity-related medical costs! This information isn't only alarming, but it also shows that losing weight is much harder than one might think. This book offers the answers to the mystery behind permanent weight loss and delves into the problems surrounding weight gain from more than a dietary point of view.

My name is Melanie A. Bowman, and I have struggled with weight for a significant part of my life. I specialize in herbal medicine. After fad dieting for years, and failing to regain my shape and health, I finally discovered hypnotherapy, which helped me drop the excess weight and improve my body image. From my own positive experience, I wanted to learn more about the use of hypnosis to support weight loss. I went on to study hypnotherapy and published multiple bestselling books on the topic. Now, I am combining the benefits of hypnotherapy and herbal medicine in my weight-loss clinic, where I've helped thousands of people reach their health and weight goals. With this book, I'm aiming to shed more light on the benefits of hypnosis for weight loss.

In this book, you'll first learn more about the true reasons why you're gaining weight or having trouble losing it. In the first chapter of this book, you'll learn why exactly is it so hard to lose weight, and what are the factors that are making weight gain consistent. Once you learn the complexity behind weight gain, you'll understand why you're having trouble with losing weight. With this knowledge, you'll, hopefully, no longer blame yourself for failure to lose weight permanently.

After learning more about the biology of weight gain and the physiology behind obesity, you'll learn a bit more about why you feel excessively hungry. The second chapter will answer some of the most important hunger-related questions, like how and why we go hungry, why we overeat, and which mechanisms lie behind binge and stress eating. In this chapter, you'll learn a little bit more about how your eating habits affect your health. With this knowledge, you'll understand your body better, and you'll start to see what specific changes you need to make in your life to lose weight permanently and consistently.

In this book, you'll also find out what gastric banding is, and what the advantages and disadvantages of bariatric surgery are. This way, you'll be able to better weigh your options when deciding whether or not to take a surgical approach in your efforts to lose weight. You'll find out why this operation is recommended only as a last resort, and why hypnotherapy, in combination with lifestyle changes, is a better alternative.

After learning more about weight gain, weight loss, and the reasons and biological mechanisms behind overeating, you'll finally learn more about gastric band hypnosis. In the fourth chapter of this book, you'll gain more clarity on what hypnosis exactly is and why it is so effective. With this knowledge, you'll better accept this form of therapy and its potential to be truly effective. As you'll learn, believing in yourself and your actions is crucial for permanent weight loss. In this book, you will learn how your mindset and beliefs surrounding weight loss affect your choices, and what you can do to become stronger, more confident, and optimistic.

In this chapter, you will also learn more about the connection between your mindset and your weight. You'll learn how your self-image has affected your current weight, and how it may be sabotaging your efforts to lose weight right. Adding to that, you will also learn the connection between being more or less proactive while trying to lose weight, and the unconscious thought process and patterns that make you either positively or negatively biased. This will help you understand some of your behavior patterns and actions. You will also learn how to use hypnotherapy to reframe these unconscious thought patterns, as well as what you can expect during and after hypnotherapy. With this in mind, you'll be fully equipped to start exercising hypnotherapy. You will better understand the importance of analyzing your belief system, particularly about food. You will also be able to develop a more conscious, mindful approach to diet and movement, which likely posed a challenge and caused a lot of discomfort in the past.

Before diving into your hypnotherapy sessions, this book will help you understand:

- How your mindset affects your weight, through the use of self-examination using the instructions provided.
- How different interior and exterior

factors framed your relationship with
food, through self-evaluation and
examples.

- How to outsmart hunger by learning to
  recognize triggers and find better
  alternative activities to eating.

Lastly, this book will give you a series of
hypnosis sessions that all serve to facilitate weight
loss. After understanding everything you need to
understand to establish full trust in this process, you
may begin to practice hypnotherapy. You will find
the first session in the fifth chapter of this book, and
it will be a simulation of the gastric band surgery.
This hypnosis was designed using a therapeutic
approach, to take you through the mental experience
of undergoing a procedure that aims to help you
reduce appetite and lose weight. With the
suggestions given in this hypnosis, you will gradually visualize and experience feeling full after eating
smaller amounts of food. This will help reduce
hunger on a physical level, helping you cut down
your daily calories without feeling deprived.

After this, the hypnoses given in the final chapter
of this book will further delve into your self-image,
self-esteem, thinking and eating patterns, and other

aspects that tailor your appetite and relationship with food.

These hypnoses will help you strengthen your willpower to diet and exercise, understand why you feel such resistance to movement, and examine negative memories and experiences in regards to eating, your body, and physical competence. After this, you will be able to look into more positive aspects of yourself and revive more positive memories and experiences. With this, and with visualizations to help you see your new lean, healthy, happy, and energetic self, you will start changing your thought patterns and attitude towards weight loss and your body. Before you start reading this book, I wish to remind you that hypnosis isn't a method to speed up metabolism and boost fat burning. Instead, it is a complementary technique best used in combination with:

- A healthy diet tailored around your body and individual needs and taste.
- A regular exercise routine, preferably one that is mindful and creative, to not only cause strain but also bring joy and pleasure.
- Medical treatments, particularly those

prescribed by your doctor, to treat other weight-related illnesses.

- Psychotherapy, preferably CBT, to look deeper into psychological and emotional issues that are contributing to your weight gain and posing an obstacle to weight loss.

I wish you good luck on your mindful journey of discovering an authentic, empowering relationship with food, movement, and your body!

CHAPTER 1: TOUGH LOSS

Why Can't You Lose Weight?

On a physical level, losing weight means eating fewer calories than you're expending. However, diet and weight maintenance are far more complex than that. What you eat, when, why, and how, is determined by many cultural, medical, and psychological factors. In this chapter, we'll review the main causes of weight gain. We'll answer the main questions behind the inability to lose weight, like:

- What: How does the composition of your diet affect weight and health? What are the foods that cause weight gain?

- When: How does when you eat affect your weight? How do eating habits and routines taught from a young age lead to overeating and unconscious (habitual) eating?
- Why: Why do cultural and emotional motivations and associations with food and the act of eating affect your weight? We'll review why you might have a tendency to eat more than you need, and how feelings of shame, guilt, insecurity, or even happiness play a role in your relationship with food.
- How: How do your eating habits and choices interact with your emotions to induce binge eating? How does eating sugary foods, in combination with emotional factors, create sugar addiction?

On top of that, we'll present you with a clear, simple description of how a healthy, fulfilling relationship with food looks. With this knowledge, you'll be better able to apply the information in this book and evaluate all the influences that are making your weight loss difficult.

Misconceptions About Weight Loss

There are a couple of common misconceptions about losing weight that keep people from developing a healthy diet and sculpting their bodies. One of your tasks in this chapter will be to identify whether any of them affect you, and to what degree. These misconceptions originate from misunderstanding the concepts of healthy eating, losing weight, and eating properly. They include beliefs or assumptions that:

Losing weight should be easy. People are more likely to give up dieting and exercising when their journey becomes challenging. Weight loss results from regaining the balance of fat burning and nutrient intake, retrieving hormonal balance, healing from various illnesses (both physically and mentally), and developing a realistic, sustainable exercise routine. It is a journey of re-shaping your lifestyle from its very core, and can't be either easy or fast. Patience, self-evaluation, tracking, and trial and error are all necessary to learn and repeat healthy thinking, eating, and exercise habits that will consequently lead to weight loss.

There is a single perfect diet. When trying to

lose weight, people look for diets that have proven effective. They forget that everybody is unique. Body type, health condition, metabolism, hormonal status, and lifestyle all play a role in one's true nutritional needs and weight issues. For this reason, even the simplest, most satiating diets may not lead to weight loss if they don't match your nutritional needs.

5 Main Reasons Why You're Not Losing Weight

Many factors dictate your relationship with food and weight gain, aside from the food itself. What you eat, and how much of it you consume, is mainly decided by the food culture in your environment and what you've been taught to believe in and associate with when it comes to food. Eating has always been more than simply an act of keeping your body alive. We have a psychological and emotional relationship with food as well. We associate eating with pleasure, ease, reward, or celebration on a positive side, or even guilt and shame on the negative side. The biggest influences on your relationship with food include:

Food and Culture

Positive associations with food form culturally, as food is used as a reward for good behavior and achievement, and it is an essential part of every celebration. There's nothing wrong with that, of course, up until the point where the food becomes the main, or even only means of rewarding yourself, celebrating, or finding comfort and ease.

On the other hand, many negative associations with food are formed during childhood, and they're hard to get rid of. If you think about eating from a parent's perspective, having a child empty the plate is the utmost daily achievement. It secures that a child is well-fed and comfortable, which means they're more likely to grow up healthy, and the parent feels satisfied with themselves knowing that they did their job well. Their children like their cooking, which is important to a vast majority of, if not all, parents. Ideally, a child forms a relationship with food through playfulness, mindfulness, creativity, and exploration of different tastes, flavors, and textures. This way, the child is developing neuro-physiological mechanisms and getting used to the acts of eating and tasting new foods gently and with positive associations.

But, when a child won't eat, either because the

foods in front of them have many new and strange flavors, or the tastes are overwhelming, or they're simply not hungry, parents become alarmed by the idea that the child isn't eating enough, and that they'll get sick, or they won't learn the healthy habits of having regular breakfast, lunch, and dinner. In these situations, parents resort to:

- Guilt (*"You're wasting food when there are so many hungry children out there!"*)
- Shame (*"I worked hard to make this meal, and now you won't eat it."*)
- Threats (*"You're not leaving the table before you've emptied the plate!"*)
- Emotional blackmail (*"Eat up and show me how much you love me!"* / *"I love you more when you eat and less when you don't."*)

A child may simply not be hungry. Children need far less food than most adults presume, but they often eat not because they feel a natural need, but because they feel inadequate if they don't eat. This feeling follows them into adulthood, when, gradually, they become adults who eat either to reward themselves for hard work, find consolation when in a bad mood, entertain themselves when they're bored, or to simply honor the fact that they have food in a world in which many starve. All these motivations further deepen the gap between what you think you should eat and your true, physical hunger, which you should use to determine what, when, and how much you should eat. Gradually, this leads to weight gain, as you eat the amounts you think you should instead of those you feel you need.

In fact, it takes less than 100 extra calories each day, which is barely enough for a snack, for you to gain over 20 pounds throughout the course of 10 years (Kaye, et al., 1988).

If you're coping with weight gain, chances are that you are eating habitually, and a lot more than you need, for a variety of reasons. Either cultural or eating habits formed in your family. In this sense, weight loss will require reframing your relationship with food and your eating habits, which starts with becoming aware of all the influences that steer your relationship with food further from the instinctive need to eat. To start unveiling these influences, you can ask yourself a couple of questions:

- **What did your parents/caregivers teach**

you about food? Did you feel guilty if you didn't eat, or you were ashamed to reject the food that was made for you? Were you taught to fear that you'll get sick if you don't empty your plate?

- **What does the food culture of your environment look like?** Is there an expectation to eat when you're not hungry to honor the host or the occasion? Are you expected to eat alongside your friends, and saying 'no' would be offensive? Revealing the eating patterns that result from these cultural influences will help you understand how to change your social relationships so that they don't revolve around eating and help you avoid overeating for social reasons.

- **What is your personal relationship with food?** Ask yourself how much you eat because you're hungry and how much habitually or for emotional reasons. Do you have a habit of making breakfast each morning, even when you're not hungry? Do you eat every night over TV shows or movies, just to treat yourself after a hard day's work?

- **What does your diet consist of?** If unhealthy foods prevail, what's the reason for that? Is it the lack of time to shop for healthy foods, or do you have a habit of cooking with extra oil and fat to speed up the process? Do you eat to calm down? Do you feel hungry when you're angry and upset? If it wasn't for that feeling, would you eat at that particular moment?

Answering these questions could help you understand how familial, cultural, and personal factors affect your diet and weight. With this knowledge, you'll start understanding how to avoid eating when you don't need to. This is the first part of reframing your relationship with food, and it is one of the easier ones.

Food and Emotions

The next step in changing your relationship with food is to look into emotional components that affect how you respond to emotional distress

(Geliebter and Aversa, 2003). Stress, frustration, sadness, and depression have an extreme impact on appetite. When you're stressed, nervous, or panicking, your body burns sugar from your blood. As a result of that, you start craving more sugary foods to compensate for the expenditure. Another way in which your moods affect appetite includes hormonal balance or, more accurately, imbalance.

When you're stressed, nervous, or sad, the amounts of cortisol and oxytocin in your blood spike (Francois, et al., 2015).

These hormones are responsible for triggering instinctive reactions to threats and danger. Under their influence, your metabolism slows down. You see, our primitive neurophysiological mechanisms are all tailored around helping us survive in a hostile environment. When you stress over work problems or relationship issues, your body, on a biological level, behaves as if you're in a state of an imminent threat of starvation. Remember, the human race developed in an environment in which food shortage was common, and any sort of threat, like a fire or being chased by a wild animal, meant expending precious sources of energy. If that threat persisted, a primal human would face a certain period of time without food.

To secure survival, our "defence mechanisms" then slow down our metabolism until they detect that the threat has passed. However, a primal human was far more active than we are today, and they expended a lot more calories in comparison to a modern human, who moves a lot less. In these circumstances, where we're surrounded by an abundance of food, but also an abundance of stress and a lack of physical activity, our inborn mechanisms become prone to storing fat. They detect constant danger as a result of stress (hypothetical threats are detected as real) and trigger appetite with the mere presence of food. With cultural and emotional factors present, our relationship with food becomes a lot more habitual and unconscious than it should be. In reality, most of us need a lot less food than we think, particularly those who work common nine-to-five office jobs.

The mental shift needed to reframe your relationship with food revolves around reframing your views on life and other people. One of the ways to do this is to re-think all of your stress triggers and question the justification for feeling frustrated. Here, you can ask the following questions:

- How did I feel before I suddenly got hungry?
- What was I thinking about right before I felt a strong urge to eat?
- What about the entire situation triggered my need to eat?

Answering these questions will help you discover the exact thought and emotional processes that led up to the sudden craving to eat. Use these insights to question every next craving before deciding whether or not to eat.

Emotional and unconscious eating results from suppressing your feelings. Most of us simply choose not to think about things that truly bother us, as we fear it could spark sadness beyond what we can bear. This isn't true.

Let's say you were to track and write down all situations that caused sudden stress and consequent urges to overeat. What were these situations about? Which feelings have they triggered? Were those shame or inadequacy at work, sparked by a coworker's comment that your report is late? Or, you found out a coworker got engaged, which could have fueled your own feeling of loneliness and mistrust in finding love after a bad breakup?

Breaking down these situations, and then changing the way you think about them, will help reduce some of the stress that follows. For example, if you have a habit of forming assumptions about why people act a certain way, it could lead you to think that people look at you in a negative light, or that they are malicious, when their reactions might simply result from their own frustrations, struggles, or insecurity. Learning to stop thinking that someone dislikes you as a person because they've acted rude, or that their actions speak about you as a person, will help you alleviate some of the stress that sparks profound insecurities and triggers appetite.

Sadness is also one of the feelings people find difficult to cope with. Sadness over loss can create an illusion that allowing difficult feelings to float to the surface will be overwhelming and unbearable. It won't. However, it's very common for people to find consolation from sadness in eating, most often sugary foods and sweets (Spence, 2017). These foods help raise levels of serotonin, a hormone in charge of inducing happiness. You can stimulate serotonin through much healthier activities, like a walk in nature, or a conversion with a light-spirited friend. Art, reading, or some self-care and self-nurturing, can also help you boost serotonin levels without the use of food. When it comes to reshaping the way you respond to sadness, you can also look into the feelings the loss itself induces and then revive moments when you felt happy and fulfilled.

For example, if you're sad because you miss an ex-partner, or you grieve the loss of a loved one, escaping these feelings while eating ice cream and watching a movie might offer temporary relief, but it doesn't offer acceptance, closure, or resolution. The sadness will come back, so practicing a response that's more accepting of your true feelings and allows you to process them and revive the positive moments that balance out the negative ones, is a much better approach.

Some of the common situations that trigger emotional appetite and binge-eating include failures at work, grief, or temporary losses of something you deeply cared about.

Let's say you, indeed, made an error at work, and your superior brought it to your attention. You may feel like you failed, and feel sad that your hard work isn't producing desired results. If your typical reaction would be to order take-out and binge-watch your favorite TV show, let's try to find a different way of coping. Instead of eating, you can think about why the events at work made you feel the way you do:

- Did something that was said make you feel inadequate or like a failure?
- Are there any negative consequences to your work or career path that resulted from this event?
- Is the situation truly as bad as it appears?

After this analysis, you might conclude that you could have, even only slightly, exaggerated the prospect of a negative outcome. After all, if your work wasn't beneficial and needed in the organization, why would they keep you there? Now, it's time to revive some of the positive memories that might help you feel better about yourself and resist food cravings:

- You probably recall doing a good job, experiencing praise and validation, and feeling empowered.
- Remember at least three instances when your talents and engagement helped the organization. In particular, pay attention to everything you did to help your

coworkers when it wasn't needed or asked of you. Most people do this at work and rest assured it doesn't go unnoticed. Even if it does, you are the one who should notice and praise your efforts.

- Recall your successes, charitable work, and small acts of kindness you did for people around you - friends, family, and coworkers. Remember how these experiences felt and how pleased you were with yourself.
- After spending some time reflecting on pleasant memories, ask yourself what in these actions and events defines you, and what it says about you. If you helped with no expectations, did good and honest work for the organization, and showed loyalty and devotion, what does that say about you? Most certainly, I'd say that that kind of a person is good, talented, creative, hard-working, and caring.
- Write these useful labels down, and take as much time as necessary to note the positives you just revived.

To take this pleasant experience with you into further experiences, even negative ones, write down how you think the person you just described would react in negative, stressful situations. Perhaps, you wish to be more patient and take a step back before responding in anger. Or, you want to stop and think about how much of another person's frustration resulted from your behavior, and how much of it came from their own stress, tiredness, and overwhelm.

When dealing with anger and hostility, it's difficult to process your own feelings on the spot, which is why either lashing out or suppressing are the exact two extremes people use. Both result in less than useful conversations, and they often result in overeating. Should you engage in an angry word exchange, you will feel down afterward and crave sugar to lift your spirits. If you suppress the anger to avoid confrontation, you will take it with you through the following hours and days, eating to calm down and find consolation.

Instead, learn how to react in a more assertive, fact-focused way, and then to process your anger with a reminder of how you are a truly good, caring, creative, and empathetic person. When facing difficult people, acting assertive means responding to the facts they communicate, rather their tone and body language.

Example

Your boss might be yelling at you, abusing their authority, and criticizing an error you might - or might not - have made. Either way, responding to their anger with your anger, or suppressing your anger, is unhealthy and useless. Instead, practice acknowledging feeling angry and letting go of it through deep, even breathing. In conversation with your boss, try to respond coldly and rationally, perhaps by asking what they want you to do to correct the work or repair damage. Try to steer the conversation towards a resolution of the matter. Indeed, if you made an error at work, the only logical solution is to repair it by either doing the work again or fixing whatever can be fixed. As the conversation starts to gain a more temperate tone, your anger will also be alleviated. Now, you'll no longer think about how hostile or unlikeable your boss is, but instead, what you'll do moving forward to correct and improve your work.

After the event has passed, you can think about

the lessons the experience taught you. How do you want to change your work habits, behaviors, and the way you talk to people to not only prevent the unpleasantness from happening again but to also grow and advance? Write your ideas down, and notice how much calmer you feel. With regular practice, stress will have less power over you, and you'll build a habit of healthy emotional processing instead of suppression and overeating.

Self-Image

Self-image is a set of beliefs about one's own worthiness, beauty, competence, and value. Believing in negative thoughts about yourself, like being unworthy of love or being unattractive, is linked with obesity. Body image relates to your self-image and reflects your beliefs about your own body (Hilbert and Tuschen-Caffier, 2004). If you don't fully love and respect your body the way it is, unconditionally, it can also contribute to gaining weight and maintaining excess weight.

If you don't believe you're able to lose weight and see yourself as an obese, lazy, unattractive person, you will, unconsciously, choose unhealthy foods to confirm this belief. A negative self-image can also get in the way of a healthy exercise routine and life-style improvements. It can produce feelings of shame and awkwardness towards your body and cause you to avoid exercising, either due to discomfort or a sudden wave of tiredness and sluggishness right before exercise. With a negative self-image, your mind will (unconsciously) defend itself from facing the judgment and scrutiny of others, driving unhealthy behaviors, like binge-eating, staying up late and sleeping in, feeling unwilling to exercise, or being reluctant to try out healthier foods.

Relationship With Physical Movement

Related to self-image, your relationship with physical movement is under the influence of things that were said to you as you were growing up in regards to your body and physical abilities (Annesi & Vaughn, 2011). Children who were motivated to try and fail rather than being criticized and scrutinized for failures in sports grow up into healthier, more fit, and more sports-oriented adults.

Those who were teased for tripping, falling, or called incompetent for not showing particular interest or talent in sports, grow up with a sense of awkwardness and shame in regard to their bodies.

This creates the so-called "movement blockages", that show in the unwillingness to move around, dance, or train. These blockages serve to prevent difficult memories associated with movement from arising. They are behind feeling stiff, unbalanced, or disoriented when working out. To overcome movement blockages, you should use a gentle approach and practice physical activities that bring you joy and make you feel good about your body (dance, yoga, Qi Gong, hiking, swimming, etc.). You should also examine the things you believe in regards to your physical ability, and question whether or not they're true.

Understanding of Nutrition

Adequate nutrition requires a balance of micronutrients (vitamins, minerals, and others) and macronutrients (fats, carbs, fiber, and protein) to fuel the body effectively while stimulating fat burning. However, this balance is highly individual.

The recommended ratio of macronutrients sums up to eating around 40% carbohydrates, 25% fiber and protein each, and 10% fat (Simpson et al.,2015).

The quantities of the foods, on the other hand, depend on your health, movement, and current daily calorie expenditure. Understanding the best diet for your nutritional needs means:

- Learning how many calories you burn each day.
- Learning your recommended meal size.
- Learning about the macronutrient ratios in different foods and how to combine them to create a meal plan suitable to your needs and taste.

CHAPTER 2: WHY DO I FEEL HUNGRY?

In this chapter, you will learn more about how your digestive system works. You'll learn why you feel so hungry, and what the biological mechanisms behind it are. You'll also learn more about biological causes of weight gain, the reasons why losing weight is so difficult, and what you can do to overcome these difficulties.

How Your Digestive System Works

Your digestive system processes food so that valuable nutrients can travel from your mouth to your bloodstream, and in doing so, it supplies your body with the nutrients that will be processed into energy. Your digestive system consists of:

- **The gastrointestinal tract.** Your gastrointestinal tract consists of multiple organs from your mouth to anus. It includes your mouth, esophagus and stomach, large and small intestine, and your anus. These organs are hollow and joined together. Your small intestine consists of the appendix, cecum, and colon, and ends with the rectum. Your appendix is a pouch-shaped organ attached to the cecum. Your colon is attached to the large intestine and ends with your rectum.
- **Liver**
- **Pancreas**
- **Gallbladder**
- **Gut bacteria**, which is an ecosystem of bacteria located in the gastrointestinal tract. It helps break down nutrients, pass them from the digestive tract into the bloodstream, and synthesize important nutrients (like iron and vitamin K) and hormones (like serotonin). Your digestive system works together with this bacterial system, your blood and circulation,

hormones, and nerves, to process the
foods and drinks you ingest.

Digestion is an essential biological function, as it enables the absorption of nutrients from foods. These foods then serve to provide the energy the body uses to function and regenerate cells, tissues, and organs. This way, proteins you eat become amino acids, fats become glycerol and fatty acids, and carbs turn into sugars. When ingested, foods inside the digestive system will be broken down into parts that are small enough for cells and tissues to absorb. The large intestine will absorb the water from the foods you eat, and undigested parts of food become stool to be ejected from the body.

Hormones and nerves are also involved with the functioning of the digestive system. When you ingest foods, a process called *peristalsis* allows the hollow organs of the gastrointestinal tract to contract and relax, moving the contents through the entire system and each of its organs. To break down foods, you first chew them in your mouth, which softens and breaks down foods enough for the digestive juices, like enzymes, bile, and stomach acids, to break them down into molecules to be processed.

Your pancreas produces the enzymes that break down macronutrients and delivers them into the small intestine through ducts, small tubes that attach the gland to the small intestine. Your liver, on the other hand, is in charge of digesting vitamins and fats. It produces bile, which travels from the liver to the gallbladder and small intestine through ducts.

The Hunger Biology: Ghrelin and Leptin Hormones

It could be that you ate only a couple of hours ago, but you still feel hungry. Why does this happen? Hunger is a psychological and biological sensation that has one purpose. It tells you that you need to eat so that you can fuel your body so it can function. But, is your hunger truly biological, or psychological?

In a world in which food is ever-present, it's not always easy to tell the difference between true and habitual, or emotional, hunger. From an evolutionary point of view, hunger is a sensation that reminds us that the time to eat has come. Oftentimes, the sensation of hunger can appear even when there's no true need to eat. This mainly happens because our brains are wired to search for food.

Nowadays, food is all around us, and we don't have to look far to find it. However, it wasn't always like this. Primal humans had to work very hard to supply food. They climbed trees to pick foods and hunted to provide protein and fats. We were an omnivorous species from the dawn of our kind, meaning that our ancestors ate a wide range of foods.

As running out of food meant literal death, eating was a great concern to early humans. Our brains have grown and developed into a more complex set of functions since, but some of these primal instincts remained. Rightfully so, one might say, as modern life can occupy one's focus to such a degree that, without feeling hungry, we might as well starve to death. Typically, our brains focus on supplying foods that are high in fats and protein. These are the main nutrients needed for keeping cells and tissues alive.

When you're done with a meal, your gastrointestinal tract gradually empties its contents by pushing the foods through the system, including the stomach and small and large intestine, until all available nutrients are extracted and the food leaves your body. Once this process starts, the so-called *migrating motor complex* picks up foods that haven't been digested. This lasts slightly over an hour and a half, after which the hormone Motilin starts inducing the growling sensation in the stomach, which happens simultaneously with the sensation of hunger.

Ghrelin, on the other hand, is another hormone in charge of hunger. It activates the neurons in your hypothalamus, which sends the hunger signals. The neurons in the hypothalamus control hunger. When they're stimulated, you'll be on the lookout for food. However, it is also possible to feel hungry between meals.

Hunger can be either homeostatic or hedonic. The first type of hunger is biological and related to the true, biological need. The second type of hunger strikes when we're bored, nervous, overstimulated, or sad. So far, biological hunger is a lot better understood than hedonic. A part of it relates to the opportunity to supply ourselves with additional foods, even when our stomachs are full.

Hedonic hunger also has a lot to do with whether or not you were fully satisfied with your previous meal. If you feel like you haven't eaten enough, or your meal wasn't particularly satisfying, there's a greater chance that you'll look for additional foods.

What Happens When You're Overeating?

Your brain controls hunger based on the signals of whether or not you're full. However, this feeling also includes different levels of feeling full or fulfilled that don't always have a biological ground. If hunger is profoundly emotional, you can eat large amounts without feeling full. Instinctively, you'll strive towards supplying extra calories, if they're available. While this mechanism served humans well during food shortages, in the era of food abundance, it can cause overeating and obesity. As you already know, we're surrounded by an abundance of foods and are way less active than our ancestors were.

In addition, the foods we eat are chemically different than those that were completely organic and natural. Nowadays, most foods contain at least a small amount of chemicals, whether it's growth hormones, food additives, colors, flavors, pesticides, and others. All of these chemicals affect the hormonal balance in the human body, which also relates to overeating.

As you can see, the hunger that doesn't directly relate to the physical lack of food inside your body has to do with cultural, psychological, but also chemical influences that affect your gastrointestinal tract. For this reason, simply seeing or smelling food can cause a sensation of hunger. In fact, you can start feeling hungry just by thinking about food. Adding to that, your body has its own biological rhythm. This inner clock relates to biological functions and hormones and could result in feeling hungry when there's no real need to eat.

When you first sense hunger, your body sends signals to your brain that the stomach is empty. This way, your brain becomes aware that the time has come to renew your food supplies. Your stomach, when empty for more than two hours, will start to contract so that it can collect the remaining foods and pass them into your intestines. This process is called *borborygmus*, and you know it as 'stomach rumbling.' When you're feeling hungry, your gastrointestinal tract starts to produce ghrelin and a feeling of hunger. Typically, those who are obese have higher ghrelin levels.

At the same time, nutrient levels in your blood, like fatty acids, amino acids, and glucose, are very low. This signal urges us to eat. However, hunger isn't strictly biological. It also has many psychological effects. Being hungry will make it more difficult for you to focus and make decisions. If you become too hungry, you might even feel physically ill.

Ghrelin isn't just related to homeostatic eating. It also has a lot to do with hedonic eating, particularly because it mediates part of the stress responses. Aside from being in charge of hunger, ghrelin also has many anti-aging, cardiovascular, and metabolic effects. Ghrelin levels also vary based on dietary habits. Aside from stress, it is also related to eating behaviors. However, it was found that ghrelin is less elevated in obese than in overweight women.

Overall, ghrelin levels vary depending on the total calorie intake. Typically, higher amounts of calories consumed correlate with greater levels of ghrelin in overweight people, but not in the obese. In obese individuals, a link has not been found between ghrelin and heart rate, blood pressure, or insulin resistance. The measure that correlates with hedonic and stress eating is called 'the total plasma ghrelin', and it reduces with obesity. While the initial function of ghrelin was to prevent starvation, it may have contributed to obesity in the environments with greater food supplies.

Ghrelin is a 28-amino acid protein that is produced inside the stomach. This hormone has a receptor called *growth hormone secretagogue receptor*, or GHS-R. Both the hormone and GHS-R are present across the body and perform a series of different functions. When energy supplies inside the body run low, this hormone is secreted from the gut mucosa. Then, it signals the hypothalamus and stimulates the vagal nerves. This increases appetite, and consequently, food intake. Plasma levels of this hormone then decrease after eating.

The link between ghrelin and hedonic eating can be explained through the system of food-induced reward. With high levels of ghrelin, one will have a preference for sweets and higher chances of eating after they are already full. This served to demonstrate that ghrelin can, indeed, induce hedonic eating when there's no real need for it.

There's also much scientific evidence to suggest that ghrelin is linked to the stress response. It was already known that those under chronic stress are more likely to overeat and resort to comfort foods. Now, we know that the hormone ghrelin mediates this process. In this case, like with previously mentioned examples, it's been noted that the response reduces with obesity. Typically, the highest amounts of ghrelin are found in lean people. Also, ghrelin relates to increases in blood glucose and a decrease in insulin levels and insulin resistance. It is also related to lower blood rate and blood pressure.

On the positive side, ghrelin also associates with reduced inflammation and anti-aging properties. It is linked with slower cell-aging. Cell aging is linked with higher mortality and a greater risk of diabetes. While lower ghrelin levels in obese people may be a good sign, its reduction also reduces its beneficial effects, mainly those that help prevent cardiovascular disease and diabetes.

As you can see, ghrelin has both positive and negative effects. This means that, when trying to establish hormonal balance and a healthier diet, your goal isn't to reduce or eliminate ghrelin, or the feeling of hunger in general. Your goal, instead, should be to retrain your mind and body for more moderate, balanced reactions. When your diet is unhealthy, and particularly with the influences of emotional eating and sugar addictions, ghrelin can fall out of balance. For this reason, a mindful diet that is based on our body's true, biological needs, and your taste preferences to satisfy the hedonic urges, is more likely to yield positive results in terms of weight loss and health improvement.

How Weight Gain Occurs: Hormonal Imbalance and Insulin Resistance

At the beginning of this book, I mentioned that many factors cause and maintain weight gain. Hormonal imbalance is one of these factors. The main reasons why hormones fall out of balance are stress, sleep deprivation, poor diet, and chronic illnesses treated with strong medication, like antibiotics. Mainly, hormonal imbalance either slows down metabolism or affects blood glucose levels. Certain hormones, when elevated, block or slow down the absorption of the blood glucose, causing it to go into growing fat cells.

Here's how hormones affect weight gain (Pi-Sunyer, 2009):

- **Thyroid**. Hypothyroidism, or a condition known as 'a slow thyroid', is known to cause weight gain. Your thyroid produces the hormones calcitonin, T3, and T4. When there's insufficient secretion of these hormones, which can happen due to stress, irregular sleep, or a long-term unhealthy diet, your pituitary gland starts excreting more of the TSH hormone. This hormone stimulates the thyroid to function properly, but it can also slow down your metabolism and heart, and cause sluggishness, fatigue, and depression.
- **Leptin**. Leptin is a hormone that signals

satiety in a healthy body. However, eating too many unhealthy foods, like processed and sugary foods, may form extra fatty deposits across the entire body, including the liver and your belly. Weight gain, in this situation, occurs because the fat itself can excrete leptin, and desensitize your brain to it. Because of this, the brain starts ignoring the signal that you should no longer eat.

- **Insulin**. Insulin levels can spike due to the increased consumption of highly processed foods or foods high in processed sugar. When there's too much insulin in your blood, your cells block it from entering, and it goes into feeding and growing fat cells instead.

- **Estrogen**. Overly high estrogen levels can also cause weight gain. Both overly high and too low estrogen levels can result in weight gain. This hormone affects insulin resistance when too high, and causes the metabolism to slow down and turn all energy consumed into fat when too low.

- **Cortisol**, a commonly known stress hormone, regulates energy mobilization, and levels. When too high, it leads to increased fat being deposited, which results in weight gain.

- **Progesterone**, when too low, is associated with depression and weight gain.
- **Testosterone**. Low testosterone levels in both women and men are associated with weight gain. Testosterone boosts fat burning and stimulates the strengthening of bones and muscles. Low levels of this hormone also cause a greater accumulation of fat.
- **Melatonin**. Melatonin is a hormone that helps maintain your sleep cycle. When the pineal gland produces less of this hormone, or you're not getting enough sleep, it can fall out of balance. When you're sleep-deprived, it triggers a stress response that leads to inflammation, which, again, induces weight gain.
- **Glucocorticoids**. These hormones help reduce inflammation and regulate how proteins, fats, and sugars are used in your body. When your body heals from many periods of inflammation, often as a result of stress and an unhappy lifestyle, this

hormone prevents the use of sugar from the blood. This way, the extra glucose supplies then go into fat cells.

Why Is Being Overweight Risky?

Coping with weight gain can become frustrating, particularly if your efforts to lose weight don't seem to be paying off. Because obesity results from many complex reasons, it's not surprising that months or even years pass before you see a noticeable improvement in your weight and health. Still, doing anything to care for your weight and health is better than doing nothing. To understand why it may be so difficult to lose weight, you should first learn about how weight gain happens, and why it is so dangerous.

It's widely known that being overweight is not good for your health. Obesity correlates with many diseases, and the exact mechanisms behind how weight affects your health are being thoroughly studied.

What Happens to Your Body When You Gain Weight?

- **Hormonal imbalance.** With weight gain,

the hormonal levels inside your brain and body change. This includes the chemicals inside your brain, which not only affects your health but also your mood. Physical (cardiovascular diseases, diabetes) and mental (anxiety, depression) effects of obesity have one thing in common: hormones and neurotransmitters. These chemicals determine how the sensations received from the outside world will be interpreted, and how your internal organs react to foods you eat.

- **Anxiety and depression.** Oftentimes, a single hormone or neurotransmitter controls multiple seemingly unrelated functions, which is why making the connection isn't always easy. For example, the parts of the brain that affect mood and forming habits work together, creating a sense of pleasure and reward for behaviors one would consider healthy. Being overweight changes the functioning of these regions, which explains the connection between obesity and depression.

While scientists have revealed a direct link between physical health and the state of mind, the exact mechanisms of that connection remain a mystery.

- **Sleep problems.** Weight gain is highly associated with sleep problems and correlates with sleep apnea. Having extra weight adds stress to your respiratory system when you sleep, making it more difficult to breathe properly. In fact, with sleep apnea, it's possible to (temporarily) stop breathing while you're sleeping. This can disturb healthy sleep, causing you to wake up and have trouble falling back asleep. This further damages your health and leads to more weight gain.

Another important thing to consider is that gaining weight doesn't only result from eating too many fatty foods. It's not as simple as that. While being overweight does boil down to excess fatty supplies, the increase of fat doesn't only relate to food take. Hormonal imbalance oftentimes causes other substances, like insulin, to travel into fat cells and build fatty tissues. On the other hand, slow metabolism, either due to sleep deprivation and an unhealthy lifestyle or as an effect of hormonal imbalances, causes energy to be stored as fat instead of being expended. You may have heard of a disorder called 'metabolic damage.' When people lose weight too fast, for example, by extreme dieting and exercising a lot throughout a couple of months, the body detects that they're under some sort of distress. Too little food and a sudden increase in physical activity makes your mind think, and act, as if you are at risk of starvation. For this reason, your metabolism slows down to an extreme. People claim to eat very little after finishing their weight loss programs, but still, continue to gain weight. This is because metabolism now focuses on turning every single bite into fat, expecting food deprivation and extreme physical strain to come out of nowhere.

Perhaps, the most severe is the link between obesity and cancer. Research has found that there are 13 types of cancer associated with excess weight, and these make up a shocking 40% of all cancer cases (Centers for Disease Control and Prevention, 2017).

While being overweight doesn't mean you'll certainly develop cancer, it does mean that your chances are significantly higher. Also, a bad diet increases risk from cancer, aside from being associated with weight gain. Mainly, it's the added sugars that have a profoundly negative impact across the entire body, from digestive health to hormones.

- **High blood pressure.** Weight gain is associated with high blood pressure, which puts you at risk of cardiovascular disease. Extra weight puts your heart under strain, which can skyrocket your blood pressure. High blood pressure also correlates with dementia, stroke, and diabetes.
- The link between obesity and **diabetes** is a direct one and is very well researched. Close to 90% of diabetes patients are also obese, as extra weight prevents the body from using up insulin as it naturally would (Pories et al., 1995).
- **Cholesterol** is another blood chemical that spikes with obesity, and it associates with high blood pressure and heart disease. When excess cholesterol builds up in your blood, there's a risk that it will clog the arteries, which is directly life-threatening, aside from correlating with

heart disease. Diet is the main
contributing factor to high cholesterol,
particularly a high-fat diet.

Sadly, it could happen that, despite your best efforts to keep your diet in check, the excess weight persists. Most commonly, low physical activity, combined with an unhealthy diet causes weight gain. However, medication, hormonal imbalance, and thyroid problems can make it hard to shed pounds no matter how hard you try. In this case, thorough health-checks, lab tests, and customized weight loss plans will yield long-term progress.

As I said before, no matter how hard and unsuccessful losing weight might feel, you should always praise your efforts. Even if you're stuck in one place, you are not getting worse, which, in itself, is valuable progress. To sum up, doing the best you can to stay healthy will prevent many uncomfortable consequences of weight gain, such as:

- Losing your sense of taste, which increases food consumption,
- Frequent migraines,
- High cholesterol,

- Depression, as a result of hormonal imbalance and a negative body image,
- Fertility problems as a result of adipose tissue-induced hormonal imbalance,
- Muscle pain resulting from vitamin D deficiency, that also correlates with calcium deficiency and chronic pains, autoimmune disease, and bone diseases,
- Sleep apnea and snoring,
- DNA changes that lead to diabetes in both parents and children,
- Urination problems, that can be a sign of kidney disease,
- Problems with breathing and a lack of healthy sleep,
- And others.

CHAPTER 3: GASTRIC BANDING - A LAST MEDICAL RESORT

What Is Gastric Banding?

So, what if you've tried everything - dieting, exercise, lifestyle changes, and you're still not losing weight? Sometimes, surgical intervention is needed to make the process easier. With laparoscopic gastric banding, a surgeon will insert a band around the top part of your stomach. This will create a small pouch to hold in food and help you feel fuller after eating smaller amounts of food. Adjusting the band is even possible after surgery. If needed, a surgeon will loosen the band, so that the food passes and moves through your stomach more easily. But, how does this surgery work?

How Is Gastric Banding Performed?

Gastric banding is one of many surgical treatments for obesity. The surgeries done to aid weight loss are called 'bariatric surgery.' While each of them is done differently, all of these surgeries contribute to the reduction of the stomach, and as a result, reduction of appetite and ingested foods. Bariatric surgeries result in eating smaller amounts of food because you feel fuller faster. Here's how the gastric banding surgery looks:

- First, you'll be put under anesthesia. The anesthesia will be general, meaning that you'll be fully asleep and won't feel any pain during the procedure.
- Next, the surgeon will place a small camera into your belly. This is why the surgery is called laparoscopic - it is done with minimal incisions, and with the use of a camera to provide insight into the inside of your belly.
- After that, the surgeon will create up to five surgical cuts in the stomach. These cuts will be very small, leaving you with minimal scarring. They will use these

holes to navigate the camera and the instruments for the surgery. Without any other cutting or stapling in your belly, the surgeon will insert the gastric band.

- This surgery is short and simple, leaving you with minimal trauma. After surgery, you will notice that you're able to eat a lot less. The small pouch created by the surgeon will fill up quickly and slowly empty into the bigger part of your stomach.

- The insert is made out of silicone that's approved by the Food and Drug Administration, meaning that it's harmless and safe to be in your body. It won't cause any injury to your inner organs or release any toxins into your bloodstream.

Aside from placing the band, your doctor will also insert a tube to it, which will be open for access under your abdominal skin. After surgery, the doctor will insert a saline solution through the tube to inflate the band. After you're done with the surgery, the doctor will then regulate the constriction of the band for its optimal performance and your comfort. The goal is to reduce food intake, but to still feel comfortable and not face any distress due to the presence of the insert in your stomach.

This bariatric procedure helps you overcome overeating while still allowing the necessary amounts of foods to be ingested. This way, you won't suffer from malnutrition, which is commonly present with calorie restriction diets.

This is a minimally invasive surgery, after which you can go home the very same day. The preparation needed includes not eating anything beginning the midnight before the surgery. While it takes only two days to resume usual activities, it's recommended to take a week's leave and spend some time resting, recovering, and getting used to a new eating regimen. After all, a sudden change in food intake will mean that you'll have to learn about the portion sizes that feel most comfortable, and the number of meals during the day that secure the best nutrition. It will be a change that you'll have to get used to, so the first few days after the surgery should be spent in rest, relaxation, and gradually introducing foods to explore your future eating routines.

After the surgery, your diet should consist only of water and fluids. You should have lean soups (broths) during the first couple of days after surgery. The first four weeks after surgery, your diet should consist of pureed vegetables, blended foods, and liquids. After the fourth week has passed, you can start introducing solid foods. You may return to your normal diet six weeks after surgery.

There are some restrictions and guidelines for who can have this surgery. In the past, this surgery was primarily offered to those with a BMI of 35, as well as people with a BMI below that if they have other diseases and problems related to obesity. This includes sleep apnea, high blood pressure, and diabetes. Meaning, if the risk of health complications due to obesity-related diseases is high, the surgery may be a suitable option.

However, since technological advancements made this surgery a lot safer, the BMI restriction is no longer in place. If you have a BMI index between 30 and 35, your doctor may recommend surgery if you have other health complications related to obesity, and lifestyle changes didn't yield any improvement. However, you will first be recommended to increase physical activity, introduce beneficial lifestyle changes, and use medications to treat your health conditions.

Usually, gastric band surgery isn't recommended to people who have a history of drug or alcohol abuse, uncontrolled mental illness, or have difficulty understanding the benefits and risks of the surgery, as well as the lifestyle changes they'll need to apply after the surgery.

What Are the Benefits of Gastric Banding?

The gastric band surgery is beneficial because it increases the likelihood of long-term weight loss and the recovery from the surgery is relatively fast. The chances of complications after the surgery are minimal, and they include a small risk of developing hernias or infections. This surgery also reduces the risks of diabetes, incontinence, hypertension, and other weight-related diseases. With a reduced stomach, you won't suffer any malnutrition, since your ability to consume and absorb adequate amounts of nutrients will remain undisturbed.

Most often, patients report an improved quality of life after they had the surgery. With the ability to adjust the band, your doctor can track your weight loss and further tighten or loosen the band if needed. Tightening the band will reduce the size of the pouch and diminish appetite, while loosening will allow you to consume greater amounts of foods.

While the average weight loss depends on the individual, people tend to lose between 40 and 60 percent of their initial weight after the gastric band surgery (Wittgrove & Clark, 2000).

What Are the Risks of Gastric Banding?

While this operation is considered to be relatively low-risk, there's still some degree of risk associated with it. It is possible to develop an allergic reaction to anesthesia and suffer problems with breathing, blood clots or pulmonary embolism, infection, stroke or heart attack, or blood loss. It is possible that weight loss happens slower than usual, particularly if there are other health complications involved. There's a small chance that the band will erode into the stomach or slip. In this case, your surgeon will need to remove it.

Some 15% of patients typically need follow-up surgery to address some of the complications resulting from a laparoscopic gastric band (Wittgrove & Clark, 2000).

It is very important to follow your dietary recommendations after the surgery. Overeating, in this case, may cause vomiting or dilate your esophagus.

As with other surgeries, the gastric band carries the risk of injuring the stomach, abdominal organs, or intestines, hernia, gastritis or stomach lining inflammation, stomach ulcers, heartburn, or wound infection. There's also a small possibility of forming gastrointestinal scarring, which could cause bowel blockage, or for the restricted eating to cause malnutrition.

However, weight loss can also result in health improvement and a confidence boost. With a gastric band, weight loss isn't the only benefit to hope for. Mainly, healing from diet-related diseases and altering the lifestyle and habits that led to overeating is the biggest long-term benefit of this surgery. For some people, their appetite is too strong to resist eating, even if it's harmful to their health. Changing your eating routine is made easier with reduced appetite.

There are also other options for those looking to reduce weight and appetite. Gastric bypass surgery is one of those options. With this surgery, the surgeon will apply staples to the stomach to reduce its size and attach the stomach to the small intestine. While this reduces appetite and food intake, it will also affect nutrient absorption. With this surgery, there's also a risk of changing the balance of the gut hormones, and reversing the surgery is difficult, which is risky in case of complications or unfavorable results.

Another option is the so-called gastric duodenal switch. With this surgery, the doctor will redirect the food into your small intestine, and after that, to bypass the small intestine. While this surgery results in faster weight loss, there are greater chances of complications.

Another option is to have a sleeve gastrectomy. With this operation, over half of the patient's stomach is removed. This leaves a thin sleeve similar to the shape of a banana. This surgery is irreversible, as the stomach is removed. This surgery is becoming more and more popular, and its popularity results from high success rates and low chances of complications. In fact, patients tend to lose between 40 and 50% of their initial weight (Wittgrove & Clark, 2000).

Sleeve gastrectomy can be done either through a surgical incision across the abdomen or laparoscopically. As with gastric banding, it might take between four and six weeks to fully recover from the surgery.

The so-called 'mixed surgery' is another option, and it includes stomach stapling to make a small pouch in the stomach. After that, this pouch gets reconnected to the small intestine. However, while this surgery leads to a significant decrease in food consumption, it also diminishes nutrient intake.

In this chapter, you learned that gastric banding is one of the last-resort options to reduce appetite. But, what if you didn't have to have surgery? In the next chapter, you'll learn more about hypnosis as a way to use your mental resources in changing daily habits and losing weight.

CHAPTER 4: HYPNOSIS AND WEIGHT LOSS

Research shows that hypnosis can be a powerful tool for self-improvement, and the answer behind it is simple. Hypnosis affects your subconscious beliefs and reprograms your mind in a way. Our unconscious beliefs greatly affect motivation, assumptions, decisions, and behavior (Holloway & Donald, 1982). Changing them from negative to positive can greatly encourage positive behaviors and help you change your relationship with food. At the beginning of this book, I mentioned that the very basis of a person's relationship with food is determined by associations created in early childhood. In adult life, this relationship is further affected by the way in which we cope with stress, challenges, and difficult feelings.

How Hypnosis Helps You Lose Weight

Hypnosis, which is a mental state in which you're open and receptive to suggestions, helps question, challenge, and alter these unconscious mechanisms. Hypnosis bypasses the critical mind and puts your mind in a state of relaxation long enough for you to become receptive to learning new things. This way, people manage to give up addictions, boost confidence and improve self-esteem, and much more. This is done by affirming new, positive beliefs and assumptions about yourself, the world, and in the case of hypnosis for weight loss, with food.

When your mind is in this highly relaxed, suggestible state, you become open to adopting positive beliefs, like that losing weight is possible for you and that exercises and physical activities can become a regular habit. Hypnosis also helps bring back positive memories, experiences, and associations that can shift your mindset from negative to positive.

When weight gain is long-term and consistent, many lose faith in their ability to slim down. This belief further strengthens unhealthy habits, like overeating and smoking. Hypnotherapy, in this case, helps you challenge negative assumptions about your competence, which is one of the main contributors to people managing to not only lose weight but to also alleviate chronic pain or give up smoking and drinking through hypnosis.

When speaking of thoughts, it's important to note that they can be both conscious and unconscious. We detect conscious thoughts in our minds, but those we don't are far more powerful. We might even say they rule from the shadows, whispering quietly in our ears, and creating sudden sensations of fear, doubt, insecurity, shame, or inadequacy. These thoughts result from both early childhood and adult experiences that could have been profoundly hurtful and traumatic, and that are oftentimes too much to process.

When distress is too severe to process, we tend to push it down into the realm of the unconscious. This applies to difficult thoughts, feelings, assumptions, and memories. However, we never truly forget them. In fact, the harder we try to suppress difficulties, the greater impact they have on our behaviors.

Hypnosis helps process and let go of difficult experiences, as well as replace self-scrutiny with empowering goals and beliefs. However, this process needs to be profoundly therapeutic and expert-led. You might find hundreds or even thousands of weight loss hypnosis recordings online. But, do they work? Most often not, because they're not tailored around processing unconscious problems prior to introducing positive affirmations. If it were enough to simply affirm positive things to yourself, it would be far easier to reprogram your mind. However, true, effective hypnosis revolves around the person's actual issues and guides them towards processing and letting go before introducing affirmations.

How to Use Hypnosis for Weight Loss

When using hypnosis for weight loss, you will question and process negative assumptions, experiences, and memories related to food, exercise, and your body image to replace them with the positive ones. This way, you will gradually change your mindset.

The State Theory of Hypnosis suggests that hypnosis puts you in an altered state of consciousness. This way, you're able to bypass conscious thoughts, which alters normal brain processes. Another theory, called the Non-state Theory of Hypnosis, suggests that people act as if they're playing a role of hypnosis, altering their behavior under the assumption that they're being hypnotized (Brown & Fromm, 2013). This way, people form assumptions about how they should think and act after hypnosis, which explains the changes in their behavior.

Hypnosis serves to alter our perception of reality. In fact, studies have shown that our perception is significantly influenced by habitual patterns (Horowitz, 2006). Because we tend to follow thinking patterns based on assumptions, memories, and experiences, both positive and negative, hypnosis can be effectively used to strengthen the positive ones and take the strength, and influence, out of the negative.

Because our perception is profoundly biased, what we believe to be real doesn't always have to be accurate. Our perception of reality is greatly affected by the way in which our brain interprets the sensory data we receive. This process is known as top-down processing, meaning that the new information overrides lower-level processes. With hypnosis, you receive new, encouraging information, which helps override and break the negative habitual thinking.

However, for long-term self-improvement, it is also necessary to first process the causes and discover the true root of the problem. First, you need to examine negative thoughts and their underlying assumptions, and then override them with affirmative information. For example, the fact that your brain thinks you need sugar when you're upset is a top-down negative assumption or process. Hypnosis can help persuade your brain that this isn't true, as it, in fact, isn't.

Reframe Preconditioned Beliefs About Food, Weight, and Your Body

Hypnosis helps you override and reframe your preconditioned beliefs. Preconditioned beliefs cause you to assign traits to objects and situations that may not necessarily have to be true. Such is the case with assuming that products are of higher quality simply because they cost more. During hypnosis, you become susceptible to questioning such assumptions. Reframing thought patterns happens through two different principles:

- **Dissociation**. Hypnosis helps you question whether or not a suggestion aligns with existing thoughts, and gradually create new assumptions.
- **Suggestion**. When you're focused on a single idea during hypnosis, you are able to bypass your critical mind and accept suggestions as if they are real. When this is

repeated throughout a longer period of time, you become able to train your mind to create, or believe in, a new reality. For example, when you're experiencing stress, the new perspective may help resist the assumption that you simply must eat or light a cigarette.

So far, studies have shown that hypnotherapy can help treat the following conditions (Horowitz, 2006):

- **Sleep disorders.** Studies have shown that hypnotherapy can be effective in increasing slow-wave REM sleep. In fact, it can help achieve up to 80% more REM sleep.
- **Weight gain.** Research showed that those who underwent hypnosis managed to lose up to 17 pounds.
- **Smoking**. Smokers who received hypnotherapy managed to quit and maintain their non-smoking. In fact, 80% of participants remained non-smokers six months after the study.
- **Addiction.** Over 90% of those who

received hypnotherapy managed to stay drug-free after six months.

- **Depression and anxiety.** Hypnotherapy was shown to be highly effective in treating depression and anxiety long-term.

Hypnosis Increases Confidence in the Ability to Lose Weight

Aside from physical, medical, and environmental factors, weight loss mindset also has a great effect on weight loss. One of the biggest reasons behind a negative weight loss mindset lies in the fact that some people simply can't imagine themselves losing weight and being slim and healthy. Being overweight and coping with health issues becomes a grim reality, but it remains the only reality they can imagine. Here enters hypnotherapy, with its ability to help you imagine, and believe, that you can build yourself up to live in a healthy, fit, strong, and vigorous body. Here are some of the ways in which hypnotherapy helps you lose weight:

Discovering root causes. Most therapists believe that our minds and willpower hold to key to achieving everything we truly want and need, unless there are subconscious factors getting in the way. Most diet studies suggest that, while weight loss essentially boils down to calorie reduction, long-term progress and maintenance heavily relies on diet satisfaction and nutrient richness. You can lose dozens of pounds within a couple of months, but how will that affect your health? Will feeling unsatisfied with minimal meals be sustainable long-term? Most likely not. For this reason, scientists across different fields, from medicine to psychology, agree that long-term weight loss requires looking into a balanced diet that suits an individual. You have your own measures of healthy, satisfying, and sufficient when it comes to eating. However, many influences keep you from understanding this and feeling fulfilled.

Forming positive beliefs. To lose weight, you first need to believe in your ability to do so. Hypnosis helps you visualize and actually believe that you can eat healthier and leaner, follow up with a diet plan, and exercise a little each day.

See the positive side. Human minds can be both positively and negatively biased. Optimists tend to focus on the positives and underestimate real risks, while pessimists only see the negatives and find it difficult to believe in positive things. With hypnotherapy, you will receive more positive suggestions, like how much love, respect, and care your body deserves. Your hypnotherapist will evaluate your issues and help you formulate your own, believable mantras that will empower you in challenging moments.

Visualization. Visualizing successful weight loss helps you believe that your vision can come true. With hypnotherapy, you will retrieve some of the memories of how it felt when you were leaner and healthier, how you looked, how much more energy you had, and much more. You might also visualize looking at your current self from the position of having reached your desired weight, which all helps strengthen the positive beliefs in your ability to lose weight.

Alleviate food cravings. Imagining letting go of food cravings and finding different ways to entertain, celebrate, and retrieve the sense of safety, will help reduce appetite. With that, your food intake will also reduce, and you will gradually lose weight.

Complementary treatment. Hypnosis is most effective in combination with cognitive-behavioral therapy, which helps you question and challenge negative self-beliefs and underlying assumptions. CBT also helps create realistic diet and exercise plans, and look into hunger triggers to see how you'll change your routines and responses to stressful situations to avoid overeating. In this case, hypnotherapy acts as a facilitator of self-awareness that helps you understand your thought process more clearly. It also helps you relax, let go of unconscious negativity, and gives an extra boost to positive beliefs you're trying to strengthen.

Mental adjustment. Existing thought patterns aren't easy to break. In addition, positive patterns will need consistent work to strengthen and maintain. Hypnotherapy will help you make small, but significant adjustments when making spontaneous decisions, like choosing to have a piece of fruit instead of chocolate.

Strengthen your intuition. Your instinctive responses have, so far, been an enemy in your effort to lose weight and become healthier. But, they can also become a trusted ally. Much like those mechanisms that make you pile up pounds, our instinctive nature allows us to sense what we truly need, both physically and emotionally. Hypnotherapy helps you look past learned patterns, and tune into your intuition, which tells you what your true needs are. It will help you sense that, when you feel like having a pizza in the evening, you actually crave connection and company, and calling a friend for a chat might be an equally satisfying alternative. Over time, you will become aware of emotional needs you were failing to satisfy, and it will be easier to discern when your appetite is true and when it's habitual or emotional.

Repetition. Hypnotherapy, much like all other therapeutic approaches, can't yield noticeable progress on the spot. Patience and repetition will be required, with a gentle and accepting attitude towards yourself. Understand that your current patterns took decades to form and cement, and changing them suddenly is not only impossible but could be unhealthy. You simply cannot persuade yourself into believing things that don't seem true, and taking time with hypnosis will help gradually build-up real-life evidence of efficiency. The more you see improvement, the more you'll believe it, and you'll trust your abilities more with time.

Relapse management. To err is human, and there are realistic chances of slipping back into old habits. Every relapse is an opportunity to, again, evaluate your belief system, and hypnotherapy helps you do this. Each time you "fail" will be an opportunity to learn something new about yourself and to show yourself a bit more love and acceptance.

As you can see, hypnotherapy for weight loss focuses more on what you think about yourself and food as a means of changing your habits. If you still have trouble understanding what hypnosis is, you can imagine it as a process of concentrating on and absorbing positive, encouraging affirmations and mantras about yourself and your ability to lose weight.

Your hypnotherapist will do this using mental images and repetition, and the experience itself will be profoundly relaxing and mentally replenishing. Aside from weight loss, hypnosis has been shown to help those with weight issues improve their quality of life and feel less hungry. All of these are necessary conditions for long-term weight loss.

Still, diet and exercise are the two basic ways to lose weight.

Here, hypnosis only removes the obstacles that make you feel insecure in your own abilities, and it helps you resist food cravings and temptations. Maintaining a long-term meal plan and going out for a jog when you don't feel like it are crucial for weight loss, and will be much easier with a more positive, encouraging mindset.

Most people who had success with weight loss with the assistance of hypnotherapy claim that it takes time to see results. Mindset changes slowly and gradually. At first, you will notice that it's becoming easier to stop eating when you're full. This is really important because one of the main problems with losing weight lies in being unable to tell when you've had enough to eat. You might still eat habitually, for emotional reasons, or while out with friends, but you'll feel less need to clear the plate.

After that, you might notice that you're developing a more mindful relationship with food. Losing a sense of taste also correlates with obesity, and after regular hypnosis, you might notice that you're having a more intense experience of food flavors and textures. This also increases a subjective feeling of satiety, meaning that it contributes to eating less.

Adding to that, having a better food experience brings greater pleasure with fewer foods eaten. As you learn to take your time and really taste foods, you will eat more slowly and get better at finding pleasure and satiety with smaller portions.

Over time, you will start to develop your willpower to eat according to a program that's reasonably the best for you, which will contribute to successful dieting. You'll no longer find it challenging to cook regularly or take time to slowly pick and choose the right groceries when shopping. Simply put, you will develop patience and greater self-awareness of food and eating. Gradually, you will start to understand not just the instinctive needs of your body but also where they come from. For example, you'll discern that a sugar craving comes from a certain imbalance in your body and not true hunger. This will make it easier to resist. Or, you will better understand that you're about to make a meal simply to occupy yourself. With that understanding, you might choose to go out for a walk or spend some time reading.

Hypnosis for weight loss aims to strengthen you in building proper eating and exercise habits. It changes the way you think about food, allowing you to approach eating in a more calm, relaxed way.

With the added benefit of understanding where the appetite comes from, you will start to develop an intuitive feeling of when and what to eat, and you'll feel more motivated to move around and exercise. Perhaps, the greatest benefit from hypnosis for weight loss comes from the ability to delve into your relationship with food and find associations with emotional triggers. Once you're able to do that, your journey will become much simpler. Adding to that, you will figure out new strategies to process challenging experiences, which is another mental benefit that adds to your overall health and quality of life.

Experiencing hypnosis, when done properly, should feel light, comfortable, and relaxing. You should zone out, but not fall asleep. Your attention should be placed inwards. Unlike what you may have assumed, hypnosis doesn't really feel like a trance. You will be awake and in control the whole time. Many people find the idea of being susceptible to suggestions scary, so it's really important to note that being hypnotized doesn't mean that someone else can persuade you into saying or doing something harmful or inappropriate. As mentioned, changes that benefit your health happen as a consequence of hypnosis gradually and throughout a long period of time. While hypnotized, you still retain your willpower and the power to make choices and decisions.

Still, hypnosis has one potential downside. When done at the therapist's office, it can be quite expensive for a treatment that takes many repetitions to show results. The price of the treatment is augmented, of course. You are paying to spend time with a licensed therapist, someone who is profoundly skilled in helping you discover the reasons for overeating and the right, genuine, and authentic strategies to overcome obstacles. Still, the very notion of investing thousands of dollars into a therapy that doesn't immediately yield improvement can instill doubt in some. Keep in mind that, by reprogramming your mind, you permanently change your mindset for the better.

While the length of time it takes to see results may be off-putting, hypnosis has another benefit. It requires addressing all of your health issues first. Hypnosis works by encompassing the improvements made by getting medical treatment, exercising, and dieting, rather than claiming it can induce weight loss on its own. Through hypnosis, you will also learn the relevance of getting proper treatment for other health issues, which will be a major motivation boost. Every single thing you do to improve your health will further show you that you indeed are competent at getting better and losing weight. This will further boost your confidence and self-image and motivate a more proactive approach in healing and recovery from obesity-related diseases.

While there are numerous benefits of hypnosis for weight loss, not all people can absorb the beneficial suggestions. Some research shows that there are those whose brains simply operate differently and can't become susceptible to suggestions. Those are typically people who are not particularly imaginative or creative, or introspective for that matter. If you're on a more down-to-earth side and you struggle with imagination, there's a chance a bit more effort will be needed to open your mind to accepting suggestions from a hypnotherapist or recorded hypnosis such as the one given in this book.

If you're looking for a way to bring hypnosis closer to your understanding, you can compare it to a sensation of dozing off, only in a slightly more concentrated way. When you're in a state of suggestibility, you can be guided towards different visualizations and thoughts. Some hypnosis includes visualizing that you're looking at a screen or a board and seeing an image of what is suggested. This way, you become open to experiencing things that currently aren't really present in your life, but you begin to accept them as possible.

It is also important to note that a hypnotic state of mind isn't something that spontaneously happens to you, or is done to you, but instead a mental state that normally takes place throughout the day. The only difference is that, with hypnosis, you trigger and enter this process willingly and purposefully. There are multiple ways to induce a hypnotic state of mind. The first is with the simulation of falling asleep, when you stimulate a mental state between being awake and being asleep. This loosens the barriers in certain parts of your brain. Guided visualizations put you in different environments and situations. By doing so, they help you imagine doing certain activities that can communicate more complex experiences within your mind that encompass cognitive and emotional features, beyond just the visual aspects of the image.

Your therapist will also spontaneously say things that don't really make sense or sound confusing. This is done purposefully, and with the goal to keep you from dozing off completely, while your guard is down. This allows deeper healing because it promotes concentrated relaxation.

CHAPTER 5: GASTRIC BAND HYPNOSIS

Welcome to your gastric band hypnosis! This hypnosis will help you lose weight, without having to go through the actual surgery. The first part of this therapy will consist of revealing the root causes of emotional eating. While doing this, you will recall any experiences related to food that might have affected you negatively, and might still be affecting you now. Next, you will recognize and acknowledge any unhealthy thought patterns related to food. After this, you will undergo a visualized gastric band surgery. This procedure will install unconscious suggestions that you have a gastric band installed.

Part One

During this session, your body will gradually learn to respond to suggestions in a way that reduces your appetite. Gradually, you will start to feel fuller after eating smaller amounts of food, similar to the gastric band surgery. As you visualize going through the procedure, and the more you repeat this process, the better will your body responds to the suggestions. You will start to feel like your stomach has, indeed, reduced, and fewer calories are enough to satisfy your cravings than before. With each repetition, the procedure will start to look and feel more realistic, and you will feel a stronger, more noticeable effect.

First, let's briefly address diets and address some of the reasons why you might have failed to lose weight in the past. Failing with diets wasn't your fault, and it doesn't speak badly about your personality. Gently release any guilt and shame associated with the fact that, in the past, you might have tried to maintain a steady diet but failed at it. Most diets are of a temporary nature and are hard to sustain in the long run. It's not you who is the problem. The problem you faced with dieting had to do with the fact that overly restrictive diets aren't effective. They deprive not only foods and nutrients, but also pleasure and fulfillment needed for long-term success.

With this hypnosis, you will virtually make a commitment to yourself to change your habits and the way of eating. As you subconsciously receive the virtual gastric band, you will gradually, through suggestions, gain the confidence and discipline needed to establish healthy eating habits. These habits will reflect on the way you eat, go through your day, and exercise. Over time, the beneficial changes will build up to support your long-term, healthy weight loss, and the improvement of your physical health.

First, let's briefly discuss your weight loss experiences, eating patterns, and your general health and relationship with food.

Recall the previous treatments you tried, what your experience looked like, and the reasons why your efforts weren't successful. Mimicking the gastric band surgery will help you create an authentic virtual experience, incorporating both imagery, sounds, and smells you'd feel while undergoing this operation. In a deep hypnotic state, you will go through the operation. This hypnosis will take you step by step through the process of this surgery.

This hypnosis will start by visualizing the experience of going into anesthesia and relaxing. After that, you'll be taken through the process of having the gastric band installed, starting from the first incision, and fitting of the band. This hypnosis will even guide you through the process of stitching the cuts.

While this process unfolds, you'll be guided to sense the smells and sounds around you. This will enhance your experience and make it more realistic and believable. This way, your subconscious mind will gradually become persuaded that what you experience is, in fact, real.

Aside from simulating the surgery, this hypnosis will include suggestions that will increase your self-confidence. After the procedure, I'll present you with additional techniques to practice at home.

Part Two

Welcome to your gastric band hypnosis. In this hypnosis, you will receive a virtual gastric band. This way, you will lose weight in a way that is healthy and beneficial for your body and mind. Remember that you are always in full control of your mind and body. The suggestions you'll receive are healthy, helpful and positive, and won't harm you in any way. Whenever you want to, you can reinforce these suggestions by repeating this hypnosis.

First, let's relax to open your mind to positive suggestions. Allow your mind to calm down and become more positive. Now, you'll start receiving suggestions to be in a state of relaxation, so that you can virtually and mentally install the hypnotic gastric band.

Sit down and begin to relax. Focus on my voice. As you listen to my voice, you're becoming more and more relaxed. Keep relaxing, shrugging and dropping your shoulders until they're free of any pressure. Look around you, and inwards, into your body, to detect any tightness or discomfort. If you detect tension, relax the part of your body that feels tight. Relax any places in your body that feel uncomfortable.

Now, I will start counting from ten to one. When I finish counting, you will feel fully relaxed, in every part of your body. Each part of your body will become fully relaxed.

- Ten. Breathe in, pause, and let the breath

out. Breathe deeply, directing the breath into your stomach.

- Nine. Pause for a second time, and let the breath out.
- Eight. Breathe in for the third time, hold, and breathe out. Now, you are feeling much, much, better.
- Seven. Focus your attention on your breath, as you breathe deeply. You are breathing in relaxation, and breathing out tension and discomfort. Your mind becomes calm and quiet with each breath.
- Six. You are more and more calm and quiet. Everything around you is serene, warm, and safe. You hear only the sounds of this hypnosis. All chores, worries, and stress fade into the distance.
- Five. You are only focusing on the sound of my voice. Breathe in relaxation, and breathe out tiredness. With each exhale, you're sinking deeper into relaxation. Deeper and deeper, until you feel weightless and completely safe.
- Four. Relaxation washes over your face, jaw, your lips. Your neck is softer, shoulders relaxed. Relaxation spreads

through your body, your shoulders, back, chest, and stomach. You are softening your thighs, calves, and feet. You are soft, safe, and relaxed. You are diving deeper and deeper into relaxation, as you breathe deeply in and out.

Your hands are resting beside you, completely relaxed. There's no need to move, you are simply being calm and relaxed. There's nothing else to do but to sink further into relaxation. Your body is opening up, loosening, softening, and breathing into relaxation.

As you exhale, your body sinks further into your chair. Letting go feels beautiful. You are drifting and floating into heavy relaxation.

- Three, your legs are becoming heavier, and you're focusing on your feet as they become calm and loose.
- At two, all of your body is relaxed. Remember you're in control.
- One. You are letting go of everything but the sense of relaxation. You are completely comfortable, relaxed, and at ease. You are sitting comfortably, your mind is open.

> You are receptive to my suggestions. Your
> mind and body are deeply connected.
> Open your mind now. Accept and allow
> positive, healthy ideas into your mind to
> boost your own resources and strengths.
> Your mind is clear and open. You look
> forward to the change waiting to happen.

You're calm and excited. This positive change will increase your life's quality, vitality, and energy. You are excited and anticipating a positive change.

You are entering a hospital corridor. You're hearing sounds of visitors and looking at medical staff. You can feel the smells of clean, hygiene products, and disinfectants. Everything is fresh and clean. You are safe and about to experience a change of your attitude towards food. You are starting a change to uplift your body and mind.

You are lying in a hospital bed. A nurse is there beside you. She is here just to care for you. She is calm and encouraging. The nurse is smiling at you. You trust and like her, so you smile back at her. She touches your hand, and you feel happy and comforted. Turn around, and notice the bright lights in the room.

You are surrounded by bright white and blue

lights. These lights make you feel sleepy and drowsy. Your eyes feel heavy, and your breath is light and even.

There are several people there, and you feel like you're drifting deeper and deeper into anesthesia.

Your stomach feels a sense of excitement that grows within you. Nothing matters but this safety and excitement about a fresh start. You are relaxed in this room, surrounded by warm blue lights.

Feel the softness of the hospital bed. Focus on feeling relaxed and comfortable as a soft bed supports your back. The nurse points a bright light at you, and you can only see the shadows of medical staff walking around. There's nothing else for you to do but relax and enjoy this experience, knowing that you'll wake up with a healthier appetite.

Something cold touches your stomach, and something inside begins to change. You are drifting away and starting to observe yourself on the bed. You see yourself surrounded by doctors, nurses, and instruments. Now, a doctor makes a small incision into your stomach, a tiny one. They are fitting the band inside. Just like that, the process is quickly over.

Now, you see the staff walking away. Everyone is relaxed and happy, and so are you. The job is finished. Such little time was enough. Now, you are getting better and better. Your mind is in full control of your thoughts about food.

Now, you choose to eat sensibly and to have only the right foods. These foods heal your body and mind. You only desire healthy meals that are nutritious, abundant in fruits and vegetables.

Foods feel wonderful as you chew and swallow. They are healthy, tasty, satiating. You only desire healthy, lean, nourishing foods in the perfect amounts. Your stomach feels light and comfortable. Your subconscious and conscious mind choose this. You feel at ease. You feel well, energized, and hydrated. You desire and deserve to look and feel healthy and strong. You have everything you need to achieve the fittest and healthiest body. You're noticing how your stomach feels full as you finish the right amount. You no longer need to eat after your stomach feels full.

You have now developed healthy habits, a healthy outlook on food and diet. You look forward to being healthy and listening to your body. Everything is as it should be. You eat only when you're really hungry. You feel the difference between sadness and hunger, fear and hunger, boredom, and hunger. When you feel these emotions, you inhale and exhale deeply.

Take a couple of deep breaths, and let them go. You no longer cover them up with food. As you're relaxing, your mind relaxes softly.

You are changing as you breathe. With every breath, you become stronger and more competent, resourceful. You are sure of yourself. You think of yourself in different ways. You know and believe that you can change your habits for the better.

The way you think and feel affects how you act. You're choosing to eat properly. You're choosing to eat with confidence and awareness, and when you're really hungry. Changes happen within weeks, as you learn to listen to your body and mind. This is the effect of the hypnoband. You are more in control. You feel right. You eat right. Your stomach is flatter. You have a calm energy. You don't desire overeating. After a couple of weeks, you feel more energy. Clearly and calmly, you see new possibilities and opportunities.

You smile with pride in your achievement. You're trying on new clothes and fit in them easily. You're more excited, and you have more energy.

You enjoy moving and exercising. You enjoy healthy foods, and the softness and flavor of protein, fruits, and vegetables. You become stronger, and slimmer. Your posture is tall, head held high. Your friends, family, and colleagues comment on how much better you look and how much more energized you are. Everything is in its place. You are healthy and happy.

You continue to believe from now on, as you allow your mind and body to consume healthy, nutritious foods in the amounts you need. If you want to sleep, drift off. If you want to wake, you will wake up energized and refreshed. You're looking forward to your day. Now, I will count from one to three. One, now the energy returns through your body, from your feet to head. Two, you are fully present and aware of the energy moving through your body. Three, you are opening your eyes. You're fully alert, and you know something wonderful has happened.

After the Hypnosis

After you go through the entire process of the gastric band hypnosis, you will gradually start craving more healthy foods. The subconscious suggestions you received will train your brain to send the message of feeling full after eating less food. If you're overeating, you will start to recognize being physically full. In the past, this could have been diffi-

cult. With hypnosis, you'll start noticing the difference between being hungry and being full. You will
start to notice small, barely noticeable physical
sensations that appear as you get hungry, and you'll
start detecting how you feel when you start feeling
full. This will set the basis for you to start developing healthy eating habits.

Moreover, the hypnosis will feel safe, relaxing,
and pleasant, helping you build a calmer approach to
reviewing intrinsic issues surrounding food, your
body, and weight.

With the gastric band hypnosis, you'll reap all the
benefits of the experience, but without the physical
pains of recovery. You won't experience any nausea,
acid reflux, or vomiting. Physical symptoms of the
surgery won't manifest, as the experience is entirely
psychological. Ultimately, whether or not the gastric
band hypnosis will work for you depends on many
factors. It could happen that you notice behavioral
changes and changes in sensations soon after your
first session, or it could take multiple sessions before
you notice any changes. Either way, you should be
patient and allow the changes to manifest in a way
that's natural to you and your mind.

For best results, it is necessary that you trust the
process, feel relaxed, and enjoy. This will strengthen

the positive beliefs being suggested, and help you notice progress faster. It will help you place your focus on feeling comfortable, and calmly accept sensing, feeling, and noticing the core issues as they arise.

On a hypnotic level, relaxation will help you to open up to positive suggestions, while on the conscious or cognitive level, it will help you rationally evaluate some of your insights. As you process and evaluate your experiences, it is possible to let go of some of those negative beliefs with the simple act of reasoning. Chances are that at least some of your unconscious beliefs may be let go of as you simply realize that they aren't rooted in truth.

CHAPTER 6: COMPLIMENTARY HYPNOSIS FOR A WHOLISTIC APPROACH

Hypnosis for Binge Eating

Welcome to the hypnosis to help you overcome binge eating! Binge eating happens when you're unwilling to cope with your true feelings. This hypnosis will give you suggestions to stop suppressing feelings and start processing them in a healthy way, without overeating.

Count down from 10 to 1 slowly and evenly. Ten. Slow down your breathing, but make sure it's still even. Nine. Relax, and focus on accepting feelings and thoughts as they arise. Don't try to change or suppress them. Some of these thoughts and feelings might surprise you, or be intense or painful. Eight.

Try to observe your feelings as if they're happening to someone else, without engaging emotionally. Seven. Focus on accepting your feelings, and affirm that all of your feelings are good. They exist for a reason. Six. Accept them and try to empathize with the way you're feeling, and with yourself, as if you're empathizing with another person.

Five. Learning how to fully accept the way you think and feel is beneficial on multiple levels. In terms of overeating, it will reduce it, as it will weaken the barriers that prevent you from feeling the way you truly do. Four. This way, it will be easier to notice when your appetite arises simultaneously with sensations of stress, fear, sadness, shame, anger, or inadequacy. Three. With the ability to notice the arrival of these feelings, you will have greater power over choosing whether or not to eat. Two. Breathe in and out, relaxing your entire body. One. Drift into complete relaxation, imagining that you're standing somewhere quiet, comfortable, and relaxing.

Now, start working on unveiling each individual feeling you might have been trying to suppress. Accept that, from now on, you will choose to feel your feelings, and respond to them in a helpful, compassionate way, the same as you would with any other person.

Focus on the feeling of anxiety. From now on, whenever you feel anxious, you will place your focus on issues in your life that need to be resolved.

If you're feeling depressed, you will acknowledge this feeling when it arises. You will understand that feeling depressed means that you need to become more proactive about solving your problems. If you're frustrated, it means that you need to change your approach to the problem. When you're stressed, it means that you need to slow down and take on only as much work as you can realistically handle.

When you're lonely, it is a healthy desire for human contact. Instead of eating, you will talk to someone, or do more outgoing activities to be in contact with other people. Perhaps, you will start volunteering, or you could join a class or a group that revolves around your interests.

Now, start to understand that eating won't satisfy your feelings. It might temporarily alleviate them, but they will come back. Now, you will choose to listen to your feelings. You will listen to what your feelings are trying to tell you, and you will note the memories of how certain feelings and situations caused overeating.

Hypnosis for Emotional Eating

Welcome to the hypnosis to overcome emotional eating. Sit back, and allow your entire body to relax. Relax your muscles starting from the tip of your head, over your face, neck, and shoulders, down to your stomach, hips, thighs, calves, and the soles of your feet. Allow the following minutes to be just for you. If any distressing thoughts arise, gently accept them and let them go.

Now, take a couple of deep breaths. Close your eyes. Breathe slowly, evenly, and naturally. Imagine floating on the surface of a serene ocean, with waves slowly washing away any tension, stress, or negative feelings. Focus on the sensation of gentle rocking, the smell of the ocean filling your lungs, and the sounds of waves and seagulls carrying you further and further into relaxation. Now, let's count down from 10 to one. Imagine white numbers in front of your eyes starting from ten, nine, eight, seven, six, five, four, three, two, and one. Now, you're fully relaxed.

Now, you will start to evaluate your relationship with food. Look back at your childhood, and bring back the earliest memory you have of eating.

Perhaps, it is alongside your family, maybe or you're by yourself. How do you feel? Do you feel happy and satisfied? Or, perhaps, you feel tense or ashamed. Take some time to reflect on your memory.

Now, let's travel into your teens and adult years. What do you remember feeling? Were you nervous or anxious? Are there memories of eating to find consolation? If there are, bring back some of those memories. Look into how you felt.

Now, ask yourself why you feel hungry when difficult emotions arise. Are you trying to shelter yourself from bringing back the trauma, stress, or sadness? Perhaps, you eat when you feel scared, and you don't want to feel scared. Now, acknowledge that you're making the choice to feel your true feelings. If any difficult feelings arise, choose now to acknowledge them.

Perhaps, you thought that feeling angry, sad, or scared makes you weak. Perhaps, even though you might not remember, there were situations when you were shamed for feeling down and needing support. If you remember any of those situations, commit to giving yourself the true love, consolation, and support you deserve. Now, you are making a commitment to yourself to honor your feelings because they are yours. You are choosing to meet them with compassion and acceptance. You're no longer afraid that feeling those feelings makes you weak or inadequate, and you're not worried you'll do something wrong and irresponsible. You are a strong, mature, responsible adult, who is in full control of their actions. You are fully capable and competent to respond in appropriate ways the next time you feel distressed.

You will now make a commitment to yourself to start processing your feelings. Recall the last time you remember feeling a sudden urge to overeat. Which feelings arise when you remember this event? Do you feel embarrassed, ashamed, incompetent, or like a failure? Allow these feelings to float through you. Now, commit yourself to fully honor your feelings, much like you would if you were consoling a friend, a child, or any other loved one. Find compassion for the way you feel right now.

Pay attention to physical sensations that arise when you're in distress. Is your heart beating stronger? Do you feel any tension or unpleasantness in your stomach? Are your limbs stiff? Are your fists clenched? If so, start releasing the tension now. Take a deep breath and state that you fully accept the way you think and feel in this moment. Breathe out and state that you're choosing to let go of difficult feelings. You are choosing to allow yourself to feel exactly the way you feel the next time you're in distress. Make a promise to yourself that you won't try to suppress your feelings.

Now, let's travel into a more pleasant memory. Recall a situation when you remember feeling completely happy about yourself. How did this sensation feel? Did you feel proud of your achievements? Perhaps, a sensation of warmth filled your chest and you were smiling. Recall a situation where you felt truly competent and happy with yourself. What did you think about yourself in this situation? Did you feel proud of how well you did the work, or proud of making someone happy? Did you feel smart and competent? What did you learn from this experience?

You are choosing to recall this pleasant experience the next time you feel down. You are choosing to remember the times you felt proud, good, creative, competent, and attractive. The next time a difficult feeling arises, you will give yourself the love that you deserve. You will choose to honor your feelings and think about their meaning. Instead of eating, you will take a walk or talk to a friend about the things that bother you. Evoke compassion, love, and happiness for yourself to the greatest of your ability. Take some time to relish in your own worthiness. As you breathe in, feel proud of yourself for choosing to honor your feelings. As you breathe out, confirm your decision to better face and process feelings.

Now, you are coming back to awareness. You are fully aware of your surroundings, and starting to feel more awake and alert. Open your eyes gently. Take some time to think about your experience, and take the sensation of satisfaction and fulfillment into your day.

Hypnosis for Cultural Eating

Now, let's start the hypnosis. First, find a quiet, comfortable space. The room you're in should make you feel safe. Place yourself in quiet surroundings, where you won't be distracted. Perhaps, you can sit comfortably in your favorite chair. Make sure to turn off your TV, cellphone, or any other devices that could otherwise distract you. If you live with other people, let them know you want to be alone and that they shouldn't disturb you.

Now, let's get ready to enter the state of hypnosis. In the state of hypnosis, you will not fall asleep. Rest assured that you're fully aware and in control of your mind and body. Under hypnosis, you won't do anything you don't want to.

Now, think about the reasons why you want to get hypnotized. What are your goals with this hypnosis? What is it that you're trying to achieve? Focus while thinking on this goal, and relax. Relax, and allow your mind to wander. If you've practiced hypnosis before, you might be familiar with how it feels. Perhaps, you've built a sensation of how it feels to receive suggestions. If not, don't force any expectations or visualizations upon yourself, other than whatever comes naturally.

Focus on the tone and voice of this session. Find a place, either mentally or physically, that helps you calm down and relax. Breathe evenly, deeply, and naturally. Allow my words to gently wash over your head, face, shoulders, and legs, removing all stress and tension. Remember that you are safe. You are calm and peaceful. You're in full control of your mind and body.

Remember, you will only receive suggestions that benefit your body and mind. You will only accept those suggestions you want to accept.

Now, focus on your breath. Breathe in and out deeply, evenly, and naturally. As you breathe in, fill in your lungs. As you breathe out, allow the breath to take away any remaining pressure, tension, or dissatisfaction. Now, focus your gaze on one point. It can be somewhere in the room or any small object of your choosing. If you want to, you can close your eyes and focus on the space between your eyebrows.

Now, start relaxing your body one part after another. First, focus on the top of your head, letting go of any sensations of stress. Follow up with your forehead, eyes, the back of your head, eyebrows, cheeks, mouth, and jaw. Relax your jaw so that it's not tense, but not too much as to open your mouth. Relax your neck enough to loosen tension, but still keep your head straight. Do the same with your shoulders and back. Focus on your chest, and relax any tension present in that area, moving on to relax your stomach, hands, thighs, calves, and feet.

Allow all the muscles in your body to loosen and lighten, from the top of your head to the soles of your feet. Now, allow the waves of heavy relaxation to come over you, arising as you breathe in, and falling as you breathe out. Feel yourself relaxing, and allow the waves to carry you further and further into relaxation.

As you listen to these words, focus on my voice. As you're gently floating into relaxation, focus on my voice to guide you further and further, deeper and deeper, into a weightless state of ever-growing softness, safety, and security. You are diving deeper and deeper into relaxation. The deeper you relax, the better you feel.

Now, you are finding yourself in a place that feels safe, pleasant, and liberating. Perhaps, it's a meadow or a beach. As you're looking down, you're noticing a staircase. As you step down, you're feeling calmer and calmer. Finally, you're reaching the bottom of the staircase. Now, you're seeing a door in front of you. As you open the door, you are entering the space of pure relaxation.

You are seeing yourself, as a child. You're surrounded by your family. The room you're in could be the kitchen, or a diner. The walls around you are decorated with the symbols of your culture. What are those symbols? What do they mean to you? Look at the table in front of you. Which foods are on the table? How do you feel about these foods? Do you feel hungry? Or, do you not want to eat? How do people around you react to you grabbing a bite? Are they happy, or judgmental? How do they react if you turn down the offered foods? Are they offended? Are they displeased?

Oftentimes, we eat to please others. We eat to be a part of a group or to enhance the feeling of celebration and joy. But, do you need to eat on these occasions? Picture yourself in this room, now as an adult. Look at the food in front of you. Imagine that this is a safe space, where no one will judge you for either eating or refusing to eat.

How do you feel? If you feel hungry, grab a bite. If not, proceed to participate in the joy without eating. Now, you understand that you have the ability to choose. Eating doesn't affect your connection with family and friends. Imagine yourself talking, laughing, and having fun without eating.

Are you starting to feel hungry, even if you previously weren't? If so, ask yourself why. What are the thoughts going through your mind that are causing this appetite?

If you want to eat to belong to a group, imagine saying something funny instead. Imagine talking to someone you love, instead of reaching for a bite. Immerse yourself in the feeling of joy and shared intimacy with the loved one. Now, you understand that you don't need to eat to connect.

If you eat to occupy your hands and keep your-self busy, ask yourself why. Are you trying to avoid awkward questions? Are there unresolved conflicts you want to distract yourself from? If so, look at the person you think causes these feelings. Speak your mind, and let them know how you feel about their behavior. Tell them that what they're asking makes you feel ashamed, hurt, or sad. Tell them that you have the right to enjoy their company without having to answer any awkward questions. Acknowl-edge your right to feel the way you feel, but instead of eating, breathe in comfort and security. As you breathe out, let go of any distress, and focus your attention on pleasant chatter and laughter at the table. Observe as your appetite is alleviated.

Now, imagine everyone leaving the room. You are alone. The room is filled with morning light. You've just awakened and are about to start your day. Your stomach is empty. It's time to connect with your intuitive self and learn how to measure your meals.

Imagine that the table in front of you is filled with various foods. You now start to examine these foods, with an empty plate in front of you. What are the foods your body craves? What are the healthy, beneficial foods that will nurture your body and mind? Pick up an empty plate, and start reaching for the food. Observe as you put pieces of fruits, vegetables, proteins, and dairy on it. What are the amounts your stomach needs? Listen to it carefully. First, you might reach for each food that looks tasty. Look at your full plate. How full is it really?

Perhaps, you've filled your plate with more food than you need. If so, look at those foods you want to remove from your plate. Are there any foods that look too fatty, or they're just too much? If so, put them back into their bowls, without feeling ashamed. Do this slowly, piece by piece, acknowledging your right to not eat the foods that feel like too much. Now, you're left with your perfect portion size. Observe your plate. What's on your plate? Which foods have you chosen to eat, and how do they make you feel?

If you feel hungry, imagine yourself taking one bite at a time, eating slowly, as you enjoy the delicious foods. Soon, you feel your stomach filling up. You no longer need to eat. You know it's time to stop. If there are remaining foods on your plate, leave them. Get up and leave the table. Look back at your plate. You no longer need to eat to finish your entire meal.

From now on, you will only eat enough to feel full and satisfied. When you feel like you've eaten enough, you will leave the table. You won't feel any guilt or shame. Now, you know it's your right to eat only as much as you need. It's your right to pick only healthy foods. Focus on the sensation of satiety and pleasure in your stomach. Your stomach feels pleasantly full, but not heavy or bloated. Breathe in, and feel the pleasure of knowing that the healthy, nourishing fruits, vegetables, and meats, are now turning into energy inside your body. You feel this energy coursing from your stomach and into your muscles, bloodstream, and brain. Feel the healthy foods fueling your body, and making it strong, vigorous, and slim. Focus on the sense of pride, pleasure, and excitement, for you've now made a change.

Look around the room, and find a door. This is the door that will lead you back into full awareness. Walk to the door, and open it. Take another breath in, and hold that feeling of healthy, pleasurable satiety in the perfectly right amount. You now have the ability to connect with your stomach, and intuitively sense the right foods and the right amounts to eat. Walk through the door as you breathe out. Open your eyes, and focus on the sensation of the right measure of food in your stomach. Remember that, with each day, you are connecting with your true self and improving your intuition to decide what, when, and how much you'll eat. You now understand that you don't have to eat to participate in your cultural and social activities. Take this knowledge with you into the day ahead.

Hypnosis for Motivation to Work Out

This hypnosis will increase your desire to work out. Exercise is important and good for you, you know it. But, a part of you doesn't want to exercise. You are waiting for the right time, the right place, company, or equipment. Exercising might seem challenging. But, with drive and determination, you will feel the drive to exercise consistently.

With this hypnosis and positive suggestions, you will create the desire and motivation to enjoy exercises and make it a crucial part of your life. All you need to do is sit back and relax. Get comfortable and close your eyes. Focus inward and let go of all stress and tension. Focus on your intention to exercise consistently and with joy and pleasure. Close your eyes and focus on how relaxed you feel. Breathe in and inhale relaxation. As you breathe out, let go of stress.

In hypnosis, time slows down. You have the time to enter the world of all possibilities in your mind. There are no limitations. You can imagine, create, and manifest everything you want into your reality. You are aware of thoughts, feelings, and sensations. You are opening more inwards and becoming aware of your mental world. You are in complete control. As you breathe, you are drifting. Imagine sitting somewhere outside, in the fresh air. It could be either day or night, whichever feels most comfortable. You're feeling safe and protected.

You are noticing a large bonfire in front of you. As you get closer, you feel the energy and warmth surrounding you. You feel a warm sensation in your muscles and warm relaxation washes over your muscles. It fills you up with healing energy that restores you inside out. This warm energy flows through your body. Your muscles are relaxing and letting go. Your body is relaxing from your feet through your torso and the top of your head. The warm energy fills in and relaxes your muscles. It softens the muscles of your face, neck, and head. You are relaxing and letting go while gazing into the flame.

These flames hold your love, creative drive, and desire. They represent your inner strength, endless creative potential, personal power, and a trans-formation.

Breathe in this warm energy, and exhale into the fire. Watch it as it grows and expands. You breathe in healing energy and passion. As you exhale, you fuel the fire to grow stronger. Count from three to one. With each breath, the fire grows stronger. You sink deeper and deeper with each breath. You are opening your mind to the warmth and influence of these burning passions, to the dreams that come true.

Two, you are more relaxed. You are opening yourself to exploring your mind and looking forward to finding your passion. One. You are ready to plant the ideas of drive and passion into your mind. Your mind is fully open and receptive to positive suggestions. You know everything is in your best interest. You are ready to receive and manifest these suggestions into your reality.

You want to exercise. You know that exercise is good for you. You know you have the drive and passion to exercise every day.

You know that you need to get rid of excuses, fears, and doubts, to rediscover inborn drive and passion. Gaze deeply into the flames of your passion and choose to let go of insecurity. Breathe out the insecurity, and breathe in passion and love for yourself and your body. Look down. Below, there are sticks and stones that symbolize your excuses, fears, doubts, and painful memories related to movement, exercise, your physical abilities, and your body.

Collect these pieces, and throw them into the fire. Toss each of these sticks one by one, watching as they turn to ash. Your excuses, painful feelings, memories, and insecurities disappear. They fuel the flames of your drive and power.

As you toss the items into the fire, all of your fears burn away. You watch them vanish into nothingness and feed into your desire to exercise. Observe each of them, thinking about what they mean. As you toss them into the fire, say goodbye and watch your love, motivation, and desire, burn them all and grow stronger and stronger. Keep finding more and more obstacles, tossing them into the fire. Focus on watching the love and passion burning within take them all away. Now, look down, and notice a small seed. It contains motivation and drive to exercise. Plant it somewhere special, and allow it to grow.

Walk around, and find a special place to plant it.

Choose a place that signifies joy, peace, love, and passion for life. Wherever you choose is perfect. Plant the seed, planting it firmly in your mind. Now, when you exercise, you will exercise filled with the passion of joy, happiness, and love. Each time you work out, this place grows stronger and stronger. You nourish this seed to grow by exercising. With each day you exercise, your drive grows stronger.

Watch yourself a couple of weeks from now. Your seed has now grown. You are stronger, leaner, more driven and energized. Your seed blossoms. Watch yourself years from now. Your seed has grown into a beautiful garden. It is a special place of joy and peace. Think about how you planted a seed and grew it with motivation and regular exercise. This garden has fruits that are yours alone to harvest. They keep your body healthy and mind sharp. These fruits keep you young and beautiful. Look up to the sky. See yourself exercising. Notice the exercise. Which of the exercises are you doing? How is your body changing as you exercise? How has your health and wellbeing improved? Look at the changes you made. What were those changes? How does exercise give your body, mind, and spirit strength and drive?

Look at yourself growing and smiling. You're

exercising regularly and frequently, and it feels good. It's healing and refreshing. Every time you exercise, your garden is growing and producing fruits. These fruits fuel your health, vitality, and beauty.

Now, come back to the present moment. Keep these memories with you and take them into the day. Changes have been made. You know the new beliefs and habits are planted in your mind. Your motivation and commitment grow every day. As you exercise, you harvest the fruits you planted. Your passion grows and feels rewarding.

Count from three to one. As you count, you are either falling asleep or waking up and becoming alert. Either way, the next time you open your eyes, you are motivated, driven, and committed. These changes are now affecting your reality.

Hypnosis for Mental Strength and Willpower

This hypnosis will strengthen your willpower and mental strength. Relax and sit back comfortably. Close your eyes. Scan your body to relax all of your muscles. As you feel the muscles relaxing, you notice increased tension in some areas. Relax these areas and let go of the tension. As your muscles relax, you are also becoming relaxed on the inside. You are breathing deeply, softly, and evenly.

You feel perfectly comfortable. You are relaxing on the inside, inside your eyes, nose, throat, and stomach. Feel how the relaxation spreads through your body, from the head, over your shoulders and stomach, to the legs and toes.

Bring your attention to the chest and your lungs. You are breathing easily, relaxing with each breath. Outside sounds don't matter. Relaxation spreads through your body and mind. You are perfectly aware, conscious, and in control. All the muscles in your stomach are relaxing, down to the thighs, knees, ankles, and feet. You are relaxed, calm, and it feels good. Take a moment, and start to count down. As you count, more relaxation washes over your body.

Five, you are letting go of tension. Four, relaxation washes over your body. Here, you are breathing out. Two, you're again breathing in, and one, fully sinking into relaxation.

Rewards come from success. But, your success depends on finishing your work. Oftentimes, you want to finish what you've started. You want to exercise, go for a walk, or stick with a diet plan. But, a strong appetite, intense feelings, or boredom get in the way.

In this hypnosis, you'll overcome boredom. Perhaps, you feel like you want to be successful, but you need more self-discipline. Sometimes, you give up. It makes you feel bad. As far back as you remember, memories surface of how you've given up and the opportunities you've missed because of it.

Focus on the environments in which the memories take place. How does this space look? Who is with you? How do the events feel?

Now, how do you feel when you are bored and ready to give up? How does it feel to break your diet after a couple of days of success? How does it feel to miss yet another workout session?

Do you feel disappointed? How does giving up make you feel? How does it affect you? Does it make you feel bad about yourself? Does it make you doubt your worth and self-value? If so, note now that giving up hurts you. It makes you feel bad. It doesn't bring anything good. In fact, you now notice, persisting through discomfort feels better than giving up. Persisting makes you feel good about yourself, and giving up brings disappointment.

What about your commitment and drive? What

keeps you from accessing your inner motivation to diet and exercise?

Notice the shift that moves your focus from the goal. What rewards would be earned if you haven't given up? You would be healthier, slimmer, more energized.

Let's reframe this experience. Imagine yourself pulling through the discomfort, hunger, and strain. Imagine completing your plans successfully. What would you have gained?

You have all the tools, resources, and abilities you need. Focus on them. Notice how your self-image improves as you remain committed to success. Notice how empowering it feels. Notice how proud you are of yourself.

Now, count from one to three. One, you are working effortlessly and easily. Two, you are working as much as is needed. Three, you're achieving the desired results. You are accessing another place, a place of success. Here, you've completed a goal.

How does it feel? Which rewards have you earned? Do you have more strength and better health? Feel the success in your mind and body. Feel the sense of achievement coursing through your mind and body. Imagine being self-disciplined.

Imagine standing on solid ground, feeling strong, free, and independent. Notice, in the blue sky, an image of what you've achieved. Notice how liberated you feel. Notice how success shines from within you.

Now, you may face obstacles or disruptions before completing the goal. You may forget the reasons why you want to complete this goal. When that happens, travel back to this place, and observe the images of a new, successful, liberated self.

Feel excited at new opportunities. Look at them, imagine as if they're real. Focus on the sense of purpose as you breathe. Accept the opportunities that lie ahead. Take this strength with you into the day. As you imagine obstacles, challenges, and boredom arising, picture yourself walking over those obstacles and reaching closer and closer to your goal. Lift your hand and touch the image. Look back and notice the obstacles you've surpassed. How does this feel? Are you proud of yourself?

Take a moment. Take the feeling of this experience with you as you count from one to three. One, you are taking the feeling of success and achievement with you. Two, looking back at the obstacles, knowing you have the strength, the ability, the tools, and the resources to surpass them. Three. Take the feeling of pride and achievement and the awareness of your ability to resist boredom and overcome obstacles with you as you open your eyes. You are fully alert and awake, feeling strong and refreshed. From this moment on, you believe in your strength to remain focused on the goal. You hold all the abilities needed to complete the goal. You are committed to investing strength, creativity, and energy into achieving what you want.

Hypnosis for Enhancing Self-Image

This hypnosis is for you to let go of negative feelings about yourself. With this hypnosis, you will release shame and embarrassment you feel towards your body and looks. You will abandon hurtful lies and fill yourself with self-love, self-respect, and confidence.

Close your eyes and look into your mind to shift the beliefs and thoughts. See yourself as beautiful as you are in body, mind, and spirit.

Observe your body. Your body holds your beautiful soul and is endlessly valuable. Fill it with respect and love it deserves. Accept and embrace your body for a higher purpose. Sometimes, you don't feel great when looking into your reflection. Now you will realize how beautiful and respectworthy you are. You will do this using your mental resources.

Your body is your servant. It acts, sees, smells, and tastes on your command. Now, you will learn to love it. Sit back and close your eyes. Focus on your heartbeat and the steady rhythm of your breathing. Relax and let go of any tension. Relax your entire body, gently breathing in and out. Shift your awareness to observe this cycle of breathing, as you sink further into relaxation. With each breath, you are more and more relaxed. You're drifting away and letting go of daily stress. You are at peace. Follow my voice and fall deeper and deeper into peaceful relaxation. If you're finding it difficult, understand that everyone benefits from you feeling good. Allow your mind to show you how to relax. Understand that you are completely safe and in full control. Imagine yourself crossing an ocean and passing into a world where your mind is peaceful and clear, and you feel comfortable and safe.

Imagine light shining over you, washing over any remaining tension, warming you with its gentle touch. It descends on your head and scans your mind, removing negative and hurtful memories. It replaces them with positive memories and joy. The light fills you with love, healing energy, and awareness. It travels down to your heart, where it dissolves painful memories related to your body and face, reminding you of the endless value of your mind, body, and soul. You are relaxing, letting go, and recovering.

The light moves down your body, healing it from pain and hurt. It washes away painful memories. You are observing that your body is a vessel for who you always were meant to be. It is ready to transform. Now count down from five to one. As you count, continue to relax.

At one, you are standing on the side of a bridge that travels into your mind. There, you will transform your beliefs to gain more self-love and self-respect. You are walking over the bridge, and as you walk, you are leaving any tension behind. You're looking forward to facing a change as you sink further into relaxation. At once, you're standing at the entrance to your mind. You are noticing behind you any negativity and self-loathing and criticism. You've let go of it. In front of you, there is a mirror. Look at the mirror. The first impression could invoke painful thoughts, like that you're unworthy or less than beautiful.

Look into your reflection, and focus on letting go of negativity towards yourself as the mirror fades

away. Now, you are overlooking the canyon of negative emotions. Remember the last time when you
saw the truly authentic reflection of yourself. Create
another mirror that shows the real you, shining in all
its beauty and worth. Feel the love and respect for
your reflection in the mirror. Look carefully, and
know that this is the one true, amazingly wonderful
image of your true self. You are looking at your true
self. Take a step closer and look at your true image,
your skin, hair, and body. Allow yourself to see its
beauty. You allow yourself to love yourself the way
you are. You are accepting the real you. You respect
the real you.

The true you stretches into infinity, and you're
touching it through the mirror. It flows into you,
exchanging love, respect, and compassion. You are
one with your reflection. Love and respect bind you.
You are crossing the bridge again, finding a fountain
that flows with replenishing, healing water. Drink
from the fountain, filling your vessel with love,
confidence, strength, and security. Look into the
water and look into your reflection. You see your
true self, glowing in health, vitality, love, and
compassion.

Each time you look at your reflection, you will
see your true self. You feel love, respect, and high

self-esteem. Now, count from one to five. At five, you will wake up. You will feel profoundly filled with love and respect for yourself. You are strong and confident. You respect, love, and accept yourself. Open your eyes, taking the love, acceptance, admiration, and high esteem for your soul, face, mind, and body into your day.

CONCLUSION

Congratulations! You've now learned the basics of gastric band hypnosis and the ways to use it to empower yourself and strengthen the confidence in your ability to change habits and lose weight. The goal of this book was to help you understand that the reasons for your weight gain and its persistence don't lie simply in the foods you eat. Aside from biological and environmental, there are also many psychological influences that shape your thoughts, feelings, and behavioral patterns when it comes to eating. With this in mind, I started this book with a short overview of all the factors that affect your relationship with food.

First, you learned that there are many factors that are making weight loss difficult for you. One of them, and perhaps one of the strongest influences, includes what you've been taught to believe and think about food starting from early childhood. As you were growing up, you may have begun to associate food with love, acceptance, and pleasing those whose appraisal means the most to you. This could have resulted in unconscious motivations to eat for the sheer validation of 'being a good child.' Next, you learned that the abundance of food surrounding modern living environments triggers many primal mechanisms that revolve around securing survival. The more food in your presence, the greater the chance of feeling hungry. You also learned that weight gain is associated with stress, and overeating can result from emotional issues we think we're unable to process. All of these conditions contribute to creating habits that most often cause weight gain, like eating too much fatty and processed foods, binge eating, fad dieting, and others. From here, you began to understand that weight gain, or overeating, are more conditioned by unconscious eating and behavioral patterns than one might assume. As this book revolves around hypnosis, and hypnosis can only be effective if one believes in it, the second chapter of this book revolves around discovering your biggest hunger triggers.

In the second chapter of this book, you learned that hunger has both biological and psychological aspects. You learned that, biologically, you become hungry once your brain detects that there are no food supplies left in your system. You also learned how that associates with weight gain. You learned what the biological mechanisms behind the sensation of hunger are, as well as how these signals can fall out of balance, making you feel hungry when there's no true need to eat. You learned that this is possible when you're sleep-deprived, stressed, or depressed. In this chapter, you also learned that you can distinguish biology from hedonic hunger. Hedonic hunger, as you learned, has an emotional background, and it revolves around gaining pleasure and calming down with the use of foods. You learned that eating for pleasure can become a habit, heavily conditioned by hormones. Habitual eating, as you learned, may lead to obesity. Eating more than your body truly needs is linked with many health problems, including depression, diabetes, cardiovascular disease, and even cancer. You also learned that you're not the only one having a difficult time losing weight.

It's quite common for one to face obstacles with proper dieting and exercise. Usually, the psychological and behavioral component makes it difficult to establish a healthy diet, while hormone imbalance tends to slow down metabolism and direct nutritive byproducts into producing fat. All of this combined makes it much more difficult for your body to burn fat. You also learned that there are many people whose health situation makes it urgent to reduce food intake, but sugar addictions and behavioral patterns make it very difficult. This brought you to chapter three of this book, where you learned about the last resort in battling excess weight-surgery.

In the third chapter of this book, you learned the basic information about bariatric surgeries. You learned that there are multiple types of operations for reducing one's stomach size and preventing overeating. Here, you learned that the gastric band is considered to be the least effective, but also the least risky. You learned that the gastric band surgery is performed by inserting a silicone band into one's stomach and tightening it to create a food pouch. This pouch, as you learned, helps a person feel full after having eaten smaller amounts of foods, which prevents overeating. Here, you also learned that, while being low-risk and quite effective, and with very little discomfort after surgery, the gastric band still carries certain risks. As with any operation, you can develop severe reactions to anesthesia, inflammation, and infections, or even blood clots. Despite being very effective in inducing weight loss and reducing appetite, bariatric surgery, as you learned, remains the least recommended measure for those whose risk of weight-related disease exceeds the possible risks from surgery.

In the fourth chapter of this book, you learned what hypnosis is and how can one use it to induce weight loss. To help you understand gastric band hypnosis, this chapter explained the psychological factors of both weight gain and weight loss. Here, you learned that changing your habits and establishing a healthier daily routine greatly depends on how you feel about yourself, and whether or not you believe you're competent in losing weight. Here, you learned that unconscious beliefs concerning your relationship with food, body image, self-esteem, and others, guide your behaviors unconsciously. You learned that you first need to believe that you're capable of losing weight to find the strength and discipline to go through the real discomfort of eating less than you're used to, and exercising when you don't feel up to it and when it doesn't feel good.

In this chapter, you learned that low confidence in your abilities comes from disbelief that becoming leaner and healthier is possible. You also learned that hypnosis can be a great way to surpass these beliefs and start building more encouraging, positive thought patterns.

In this chapter, you learned that hypnosis isn't always therapist-induced, but rather a common state of mind that resembles dozing off in moments of boredom and solitude. You learned that, in order to undergo hypnosis, you first need to be susceptible to suggestions, which is done with concentrated relaxation. You also learned that not all people are equally able to receive hypnotherapy.

Hypnotherapy, as you learned, relies on lowering one's guard and relaxing enough to receive positive suggestions, but still being awake and alert as this is needed for hypnosis to be successful. You learned that, when you're in a hypnotized state of mind, your mind is more open and receptive to learning positive, encouraging beliefs to override the old, negative ones. You learned that, prior to receiving hypnotherapy, one must examine their belief system to determine the goals of the treatment and the suggestions that are best suited to each individual's belief system. You learned that hypnotic suggestions, when received regularly and throughout a long period of time, can help you reframe the ways you look at your life, diet, body, and self-value. You learned that hypnotherapy has many recorded weight-loss benefits, including appetite reduction and a boost in confidence and motivation.

Finally, this book gave you two sets of hypnosis sessions for different occasions and purposes. The fifth chapter of this book provided gastric band hypnosis. The purpose of this hypnosis was to help you mentally go through the entire experience of going through a gastric band surgery. With the suggestions received in this hypnosis, you will gradually start to feel as if your capacity to eat is truly reduced, which will have long-term, beneficial effects on your appetite and eating habits.

Finally, the sixth chapter of this book provided additional hypnosis for self-image, relationship with food, and for reprogramming habits and behaviors that aren't helpful in losing weight. With these hypnoses, you'll find a way to address whatever issue you may have, identify negative assumptions behind discouraging thoughts and replace them with positive, empowering ones. By doing this regularly, you'll find it easier to eat well and in alignment with the true nutritional needs of your body. You will also develop a more aware, mindful relationship with food, which will contribute to greater pleasure and satisfaction while eating.

Thank you for starting this journey! I want to leave you with a final message to be truly gentle and patient with yourself while reframing your mindset. Acceptance and patience will help bypass cognitive barriers to changing your thinking patterns, which will further support your therapy and the effects of daily weight loss hypnosis.

If you found the information given in this book useful and beneficial, please leave a favorable review. It will help spread the word about your experience to a greater number of people who need help and support in weight loss.

REFERENCES

- Annesi, J. J., & Vaughn, L. L. (2011). Relationship of exercise volume with change in depression and its association with self-efficacy to control emotional eating in severely obese women. *Advances in preventive medicine*, 2011.
- Brown, D. P., & Fromm, E. (2013). *Hypnotherapy and hypnoanalysis*. Routledge.
- Centers for Disease Control and Prevention. (2017). Cancers associated with overweight and obesity make up 40 percent of cancers diagnosed in the United States 2017.
- Geliebter, A., & Aversa, A. (2003). Emotional eating in overweight, normal

weight, and underweight individuals. *Eating behaviors*, 3(4), 341-347.

- François, M., Schaefer, J. M., Bole-Feysot, C., Déchelotte, P., Verhulst, F. C., & Fetissov, S. O. (2015). Ghrelin-reactive immunoglobulins and anxiety, depression and stress-induced cortisol response in adolescents. The TRAILS study. *Progress in Neuro-Psychopharmacology and Biological Psychiatry*, 59, 1-7.

- Hilbert, A., & Tuschen-Caffier, B. (2004). Body image interventions in cognitive-behavioural therapy of binge-eating disorder: a component analysis. *Behaviour research and therapy*, 42(11), 1325-1339.

- Holloway, E. L., & Donald, K. M. (1982). Self-hypnosis to self-improvement: A group approach. *Journal for Specialists in Group Work*, 7(3), 199-208.

- Horowitz, S. (2006). Realizing the benefits of hypnosis: Clinical research and medical applications. *Alternative & Complementary Therapies*, 12(2), 86-92.

- Kaye, W. H., Gwirtsman, H. E., Obarzanek, E., & George, D. T. (1988). Relative importance of calorie intake needed to gain weight and level of physical activity in anorexia nervosa. *The American journal of clinical nutrition*, 47(6), 989-994.

- Pi-Sunyer, X. (2009). The medical risks of obesity. *Postgraduate Medicine*, 121(6), 21-33.

- Pories, W. J., Swanson, M. S., MacDonald, K. G., Long, S. B., Morris, P. G., Brown, B. M., ... & Dolezal, J. M. (1995). Who would have thought it? An operation proves to be the most effective therapy for adult-onset diabetes mellitus. *Annals of Surgery*, 222(3), 339.

- Simpson, S. J., Le Couteur, D. G., & Raubenheimer, D. (2015). Putting the balance back in diet. *Cell*, 161(1), 18-23.

- Spence, C. (2017). Comfort food: A review. *International journal of gastronomy and food science*, 9, 105-109.

- Wittgrove, A. C., & Clark, G. W. (2000). Laparoscopic gastric bypass, Roux en-Y-500 patients: technique and results, with 3-60 month follow-up. *Obesity Surgery*, 10(3), 233-239.